SHARE

Your

PARAGRAPH

2nd Edition

D0144471

An Interactive Approach To Writing

GEORGE M. ROOKS

UNIVERSITY OF CALIFORNIA, DAVIS

PRENTICE HALL REGENTS
A VIACOM COMPANY
Upper Saddle River, NJ 07458

Rooks, George.
    Share your paragraph : an interactive approach to writing
    / George M. Rooks. -- 2nd ed.
        p.   cm.
    ISBN 0-13-660796-9
    1. English language--Paragraphs.   2. English language--Textbooks
for foreign speakers.   3. Report writing.   I. Title.
PE1439.R66 1988b
428.2'4--dc21
                                                   98-22319
                                                     CIP

Publisher: *Mary Jane Peluso*
Acquisitions Editor: *Sheryl Olinsky*
AVP/Director of Production and Manufacturing: *Aliza Greenblatt*
Executive Managing Editor: *Dominick Mosco*
Development, Interior Design,
    Electronic Production: *Noël Vreeland Carter*
Manufacturing Manager: *Ray Keating*
Art Director: *Merle Krumper*
Cover Design: *Susan Newman Design Inc.*
Art Production/Scanning: *Ken Liao, Steven Greydanus*
Photo Research: *Noël Vreeland Carter*

Photo Credits:
Paragraph 1: Page 1, Vivian Garcia, Page 10 (top left and bottom right) Renée Dugan, (top right, center) Aliza Greenblatt, (bottom left) Wendy Wolf; *Paragraph 2:* Page 11, Aliza Greenblatt, Page 20 (clockwise from top left) Charles Durán, Christine Mann, Renée Dugan, Merle Krumper, Ray Keating, (center) Dominick Mosco; *Paragraph 3:* Page 21, Wendy Wolf; *Paragraph 4:* Page 30, Wendy Wolf; *Paragraph 5:* Page 38, (clockwise from top left) Rachel Baumann, Melene Kubat (3 photos); *Paragraph 6:* Page 48 (clockwise from top left) Dominick Mosco, Renée Dugan (2 photos), Paula Williams, (center) Janet Johnston, *Four Generations of a Family*; *Paragraph 7:* Page 58, Simon & Schuster/PH College; *Paragraph 8:* Page 65, Tom Watson/S&S Merrill Education, Page 73, (top left) Scott Cunningham/S&S Merrill Education, (bottom left) Rhoda Sidney, (top right) KS Studios/S&S Merrill Education, (bottom right) Laima E. Druskis/S&S/PH College; *Paragraph 9:* Page74, Noël Vreeland Carter; *Paragraph 10:* Page 83, (top) Aliza Greenblatt, (bottom) Renée Dugan; *Paragraph 11:* Page 92, Ray Keating; *Paragraph 12:* Page 101, Christine Mann; *Paragraph 13:* Page 111, Wendy Wolf; *Paragraph 14:* Page 120, (top left, center, bottom right) Sheryl Olinsky (top right) Wendy Wolf, (bottom left) Dave Dickey; *Paragraph 15:* Page 128, Center for Disease Control and Prevention CDC; *Paragraph 16:* Page 137, Christine Mann; *Paragraph 17:* Page 146, Michal Heron/S&S/PH College; *Paragraph 18:* Page 154, David M. Clark; *Paragraph 19:* Page 163, Sheryl Olinsky; *Paragraph 20:* Page 172 (top left) Dominick Mosco, (bottom right) Janet Johnston, Noël Vreeland Carter (three photos), Page 180, (top left) Sheryl Olinsky, (left center) John Isaac/United Nations, (bottom right) Christine Mann, Noël Vreeland Carter (three photos).

© 1999 by PRENTICE HALL REGENTS
Prentice-Hall, Inc.
A Simon & Schuster Company
Upper Saddle River, New Jersey 07458

Printed in the United States of America
10 9 8 7 6 5 4 3 2 1

0-13-660796-9

Prentice-Hall International (UK) Limited, *London*
Prentice-Hall of Australia Pty. Limited, *Sydney*
Prentice-Hall of Canada Inc. *Toronto*
Prentice-Hall Hispanoamericana, S.A., *Mexico*
Prentice-Hall of India Private Limited, *New Delhi*
Prentice-Hall of Japan, Inc. *Tokyo*
Simon & Schuster Asia Pte. Ltd., *Singapore*
Editora Prentice-Hall do Brasil, Ltda., *Rio de Janeiro*

I dedicate this book to my wife, Hila,
for her unending inspiration, love, and support.

Contents

Preface ix

To the Teacher xi

Paragraph 1 — Write about yourself. 1

Focus: Present tense (*be*)

Exercises: Verbs
Punctuation and capitalization

Paragraph 2 — Write about your father, or an older male relative. 11

Focus: Present tense (*be*)

Exercises: Pronouns
Punctuation and capitalization

Paragraph 3 — Write about your classmate. 21

Focus: Present tense (*be*)

Exercises: Verbs and pronouns
Compound sentences
Adjectives and nouns

Paragraph 4 — Write about the place where you live. 30

Focus: Present tense (*have*)

Exercises: Verbs
Punctuation and capitalization

Paragraph 5 — Write about your home city and its people. 38

Focus: Present tense (*have* and *be*)

Exercises: Verbs
Compound sentences
Articles

Paragraph 6   *Write about what your classmate's mother does every day.*   48

Focus: Present tense (third-person singular)

Exercises: Verbs
              Punctuation and capitalization
              Prepositions of time
              Sentence order

Paragraph 7   *Write about what you are doing right now.*   58

Focus: Present continuous tense

Exercises: Verbs
              Prepositions of space and direction

Paragraph 8   *Write about your best or worst former teacher.*   65

Focus: Past tense (*be*)

Exercises: Verbs
              Punctuation and capitalization
              Compound sentences
              Pronouns

Paragraph 9   *Write about what you did last weekend, or on a recent trip.*   74

Focus: Past tense (regular and irregular verbs)

Exercises: Complex sentences
              Prepositions

Paragraph 10   *Write about your classmate's best childhood friend.*   83

Focus: Past tense (irregular verbs)

Exercises: Pronouns
              Punctuation and verbs
              Articles

Paragraph *11* *Write about how you spent a special summer.* **92**

Focus: Past tense (irregular verbs)

Exercises: Prepositions
Subordinate clauses
Sentence order

Paragraph *12* *Write about your most frightening experience.* **101**

Focus: Past continuous tense

Exercises: Verbs
Punctuation, capitalization, and articles
Complex sentences

Paragraph *13* *Write about a funny experience you had.* **111**

Focus: Past continuous tense

Exercises: Prepositions

Paragraph *14* *Write about what you are going to do this weekend.* **120**

Focus: Future tense (*going to*)

Exercises: Prepositions
Subordinate clauses

Paragraph *15* *Describe how the world will be in 2100.* **128**

Focus: Future tense (*will*)

Exercises: *That* clauses
Punctuation and capitalization
Verbs

Paragraph 16   *Write about your last three months.*   137

Focus: Present perfect tense

Exercises: Verbs
Prepositions and articles
Compound sentences

Paragraph 17   *Write about what makes a good person.*   146

Focus: *Must*

Exercises: Verbs
Transitions
Punctuation and capitalization

Paragraph 18   *Write about your country.*   154

Focus: *Should*

Exercises: Prepositions and articles
Subordinate clauses
Adjectives

Paragraph 19   *Write about the person you want to marry, or to whom you are married.*   163

Focus: *Should* and *must*

Exercises: Articles
Relative clauses
Punctuation and capitalization

Paragraph 20   *Write about your life at age 75.*   172

Focus: *Would like*

Exercises: Verbs
Punctuation and capitalization
Infinitives

Preface

Since **Share Your Paragraph** first appeared, it has been used successfully in composition classes around the world by teachers of high beginning and low intermediate students. I would like to thank all of those teachers and students who have provided ideas for ways to improve the text, and would like to encourage future teachers and students to do the same.

The warm way in which the book has been received is directly attributable to two qualities which this second edition has retained and enhanced: a provocative, concise process approach to writing, and a setting in which *the students' own writing is the central focus of the writing class.*

What is new in the second edition?

1. One Paragraph unit has been removed and a new one added.
2. The photographs which introduce each Paragraph have been changed and enlivened.
3. The *Prewriting* sections have been lengthened with the addition of vocabulary and communicative activities.
4. Some of the activities in the *Editing* section have been removed.
5. A new *Expanding* section has been added to each Paragraph unit to provide students with ways of extending what they have learned and talked about.

Each Paragraph in this new edition has six parts: Prewriting, Writing, Sharing, Revising, Editing, and Expanding. Before the *Prewriting* section, students are asked to discuss a picture (or pictures) related to the model paragraph. In the *Prewriting* section, students read and analyze a model paragraph, discuss vocabulary related to the paragraph, and engage in conversation related to the paragraph. After this conversation, students are asked to cluster their own ideas about the assigned topic. In the *Writing* section, students transform their clusters into sentence-paragraph form, concentrating on ideas, not grammar. The *Sharing* section then calls for students to exchange what has been written so far with one or more classmates. Next, students *revise* their paragraphs using the ideas gained from other class members. In the *Editing* section which follows, students are asked to complete some exercises that have relevance to the topic at hand. After students have edited their own paragraphs using ideas gained from the completed exercises, edited paragraphs are submitted to the teacher for evaluation. Finally, the class undertakes the *Expanding* section which extends the topic either individually or collectively beyond work that was previously done.

It is important to realize that **Share Your Paragraph** is also organized according to verb tenses. It is meant to be used in conjunction with, or to complement, the grammar class. The *Editing* section of each unit is devoted to work in such areas as verbs, pronouns, prepositions, articles, adjectives, compound sentences, subordinate clauses, and relative clauses. Particular attention is paid to punctuation and capitalization. Of course, the teacher is encouraged to bring to class whatever supplemental material is deemed appropriate. Nevertheless, the author feels strongly that such material, as well as the exercises in the *Editing* section, should be of secondary importance. After all, writing is more than grammar; it is *communication*.

As always, flexibility is crucial. Every class is different, as is every teacher. Ultimately this book seeks to provide a lucid, stimulating introduction to writing for the student, and an enjoyable resource for the teacher.

George Rooks
University of California, Davis

To the Teacher

There are twenty paragraph units. It is suggested that each unit consume four to five hours of class time as follows:

Hour 1 discussion of the photograph; discussion of the model paragraph; discussion of vocabulary; conversational activity; clustering of ideas

Hour 2 completion of the the *Writing* and *Revising* sections

Hour 3 completion of the *Editing* section, and submission of the final edited version of the paragraph

Hour 4 discussion of, and comparison of, paragraphs produced— with possible final revision and editing based on teacher's comments and evaluation

Hour 5 completion of *Expanding* section

General notes:

1. Discussion of vocabulary in the *Prewriting* section should not be limited to the vocabulary exercises provided. Other vocabulary should be provided to the students as the teacher feels appropriate.

2. Students have a tendency to want to rush through conversational activities as well as the *Sharing* and *Revising* sections. Teachers should stress the value of these activities, and encourage students to proceed through them slowly and thoughtfully.

3. The students' final editing (before teacher evaluation) should be done with an eye toward remedying problems evidenced in previous writing. This focus should be provided by the teacher.

4. There is no substitute for comparison of student writing. If possible, the teacher should make copies of at least three or four paragraphs per unit and distribute them for class discussion.

Paragraph
1

Write about yourself.

The man in the picture is Oscar Alvarado. What do you think about him? How old is he? What is his job? Is he friendly? What kind of family do you think he has?

Prewriting

Oscar Alvarado wrote this paragraph. What does he write about himself? What ideas does he communicate to you? What do you think about Oscar?

I am Oscar Alvarado. I am 21 years old. I am a little fat, but I am very handsome! I am 1.72 meters tall, and my weight is 80 kg. My hair is black and short. My blue eyes are beautiful. I am a Venezuelan. I am from Caracas. In Caracas, I am an engineering student at Bolívar University, the best university in Venezuela. Now I am an English student in the United States. I am happy here, but I miss my girlfriends, Carolina, Marilia, and Marta, very much!

This drawing is a cluster. Oscar Alvarado made it before he wrote his paragraph. Fill in the empty places on the cluster with information from the paragraph. What information is not in the paragraph?

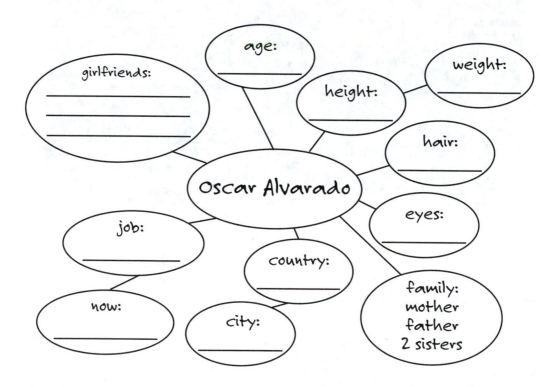

Think about vocabulary. What kinds of vocabulary words did Oscar use when he wrote his paragraph? Look at the following vocabulary headings. Work with your class to add more words you know to the lists:

BODY PARTS

hair

eyes

_____

_____

_____

_____

BODY SHAPES

tall

a little fat

_____

_____

_____

_____

HAIR COLORS

black

_____

_____

_____

_____

_____

EYE COLORS

blue

_____

_____

_____

_____

_____

FAMILY MEMBERS

mother

father

sister

_____

_____

_____

MAJORS

engineering

_____

_____

_____

_____

_____

④ Paragraph 1

Now, think about yourself. What information would you like to communicate about yourself? What do you think of when you think of yourself? Talk about yourself with one of your classmates. Then ask your classmate these questions about himself or herself:

What's your name?

What's your favorite music? Sport? Food?

Where are you from?

What's your job?

How tall are you?

Who's your best friend?

What color are your eyes and hair?

Why do you want to study English?

How old are you?

Describe your family.

Tell me something unusual about yourself.

What are three things you like to do?

Think of questions yourself and write them below.

_____?

_____?

_____?

_____?

_____?

   Think about your conversation. What did you say about yourself? What other things about you are important? Make a big cluster about yourself.

Writing

Now use your cluster to write a paragraph about yourself. This paragraph is *not* for your teacher. It is for you to share with your classmates. Feel free to make changes as you write. Don't worry about grammar at this point.

_____

_____

_____

_____

_____

_____

_____

_____

_____

_____

_____

_____

_____

_____

Sharing

Read your paragraph to a small group of your classmates or to one of your classmates (you may read it more than once, and you may give it to them to read). Ask them what they think about your paragraph. Do they understand everything? Is there anything they don't understand? Ask them for at least one more piece of information that they would like to see in your paragraph.

After your classmates give their opinions, read your paragraph again. Is there anything you want to change? How can you communicate your ideas more clearly?

Revising

Rewrite your paragraph. Change anything you want. You may change words, phrases, sentences, or the whole paragraph. You may add, subtract, or reorder. Study the following example. Oscar Alvarado wrote it before he wrote the paragraph on page 2. Look back at that paragraph. What changes did Oscar make? Why did he make them? What did he add, subtract, and reorder?

My name is Oscar Alvarado. Now I am an English student in the United States. I am a Venezuelan. I am from Caracas. My father is a lawyer in Caracas. In Caracas, I am a student at Bolívar University. I am 21 years old. I am fat, but I am handsome. I am 1.72 meters tall, and my weight is 80 kg. My hair is black and short. My blue eyes are beautiful. I miss my girlfriends, Carolina, Marilia, and Marta, very much!

Now revise your paragraph.

_____

_____

_____

_____

_____

_____

_____

_____

_____

_____

_____

Editing

Now is the time to pay attention to the grammar in your paragraph. Study the following exercises and complete them. Think about them in connection with your paragraph

Exercise A: Using present-tense verbs

Directions: Fill in each space using **am, is,** or **are.**

My name _____ Ling-Chen Chu. I _____ a Chinese
1   2

student from the People's Republic of China. I _____ from
3

Shanghai. I _____ a secondary school physics teacher in
4

Beijing. I _____ married. My husband _____ an elementary
5   6

school English teacher. We have one daughter. Her name

_____ Ruey-ling. I _____ 27 years old. I _____ short and
7   8   9

thin. My hair and my eyes _____ black. I don't think that my
10

appearance _____ important.
11

Exercise B: Using punctuation and capitalization

> *Directions:* Sentences start with **capital letters** and end with **periods.** Add punctuation to the following paragraph and correct the capitalization.

> *Example:* <u>I</u> am Oscar Alvarado<u>.</u>

i am Oscar Alvarado i am 21 years old i am a little fat, but i am very handsome i am 1.72 meters tall, and my weight is 80 kg my hair is black and short my blue eyes are beautiful i am a Venezuelan i am from Caracas in Caracas, i am an engineering student at Bolívar University, the best university in Venezuela now i am an English student in the United States i am happy here, but i miss my girlfriends, Carolina, Marilia, and Marta, very much

Now edit your paragraph. If necessary, make changes in grammar, punctuation, word order, and any other item; then give the edited paragraph to your teacher.

Expanding

Pretend you are one of the people in the pictures below. Write a paragraph about yourself. Describe yourself, your job, and what you like to do. Use the same writing process as you did before.

Write about your father, or an older male relative.

Look at the picture. Does this man look like your father or another older relative? How is he similar? How is he different? What do you think about the man in the picture?

Prewriting

Khadija Al-Tamimi wrote this paragraph about her father. What kind of father is Mr. Al-Tamimi? How does Khadija feel about him? How does she communicate her ideas and feelings?

> My father is Mohammed Al-Tamimi. He is about 45 years old. He is tall and thin. I don't know exactly how tall he is, and I don't know how much he weighs. He has black hair, and a moustache. He is a car dealer in Riyadh, Saudi Arabia. He sells Mercedes Benz and Porsche cars. His company is large. More than 50 people work for him. My father is very smart. I love my father, but I don't see him a lot. Usually he is at his company or with my brothers. I think that he is the best father in the world to his fifteen children.

Khadija made the following cluster about her father. Fill in the empty places in the cluster. Look at the information she did *not* use. Why do you think she didn't use some of the information?

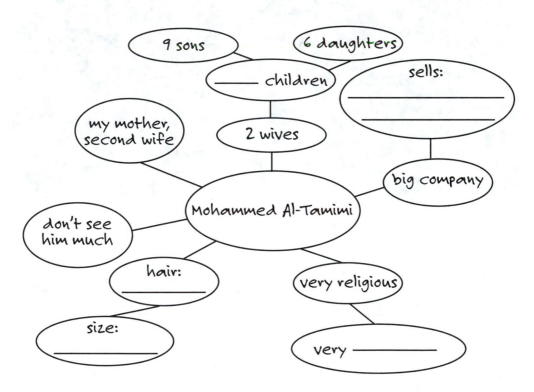

Think about vocabulary. Organize the following words into the appropriate boxes below. Working with your class, add more words to each box.

bright	big	huge	approximately	sometimes
✔ car dealer	around	often	salesperson	tremendous
enormous	nearly	almost	✔ about	clever
wise	teacher	✔ smart	intelligent	always
✔ usually	✔ large	lawyer	occasionally	businessperson

PROFESSIONS

car dealer
_____
_____
_____
_____
_____

MIND WORDS

smart
_____
_____
_____
_____
_____

SIZE WORDS

large
_____
_____
_____
_____
_____

FREQUENCY WORDS

usually
_____
_____
_____
_____
_____

WORDS OF APPROXIMATION

about
_____
_____
_____
_____
_____

14 *Paragraph 2*

Talk with a classmate. Discuss your father or another older male relative. What feelings and ideas come into your mind? Use these questions to guide you.

What's his name?

What does he look like?

How old is he?

Describe his family?

What's his job?

What does he like to do in his free time?

What's the best part of his personality?

What's the worst part of his personality?

What do you enjoy doing with him?

Write your notes below.

_____

_____

_____

_____

_____

_____

_____

_____

_____

_____

_____

_____

_____

_____

_____

Think about your conversation. Is there any other important information about your father or other older male relative? Make a cluster about him. Include all important information.

his name:

_____

Writing

Use the cluster to write a paragraph about your father or other older male relative. You don't have to use the entire cluster, and you may add information not in the cluster. Remember, this is not for your teacher. It is for you to share with your classmates.

_____

_____

_____

_____

_____

_____

_____

_____

_____

_____

_____

_____

_____

_____

Sharing

Read your paragraph to a small group of your classmates or to one of your classmates (you may read it more than once, and you may give it to them to read). Ask them what they think about your paragraph. Do they understand everything? Is there anything they don't understand? Ask them for at least one more piece of information that they would like to see in your paragraph.

After your classmates give their opinions, read your paragraph again. Decide what you want to change. How can you communicate your ideas more clearly?

Revising

Rewrite your paragraph. Change anything you want. You may change words, phrases, sentences, or the whole paragraph. You may add, subtract, or reorder.

_____

_____

_____

_____

_____

_____

_____

_____

_____

_____

_____

_____

_____

_____

Editing

Study the following exercises and complete them as quickly as possible. Think about them in connection with your paragraph.

Exercise A: Using pronouns

Directions: Fill in each space using **he, my,** or **his.**

_____ is Osman Hersey. _____ is about 58 years old.
   1   2

_____ is about 1.7 meters tall, and _____ weight is about
   3   4

65 kg. _____ is a vegetable farmer near Mogadiscio,
          5

Somalia. _____ farm has at least 100 hectares. In addition to
            6

me, _____ father has six children, four daughters, and two
       7

sons. _____ works hard to give us a good life. _____ wants
         8   9

_____ children to work hard too. _____ always tells me to
   10   11

do _____ best.
      12

Exercise B: Using punctuation and capitalization

Directions: Names of people, cities, countries, and companies begin with **capital letters**. Put a period ._ at the end of each sentence. Put a comma _, when two sentences are connected. Punctuate the following paragraph and correct the capitalization.

Example: I don't know how old he is _, and I'm not sure how tall he is ._

my father is mohammed al-tamimi he is about 45 years old he is tall and thin i don't know exactly how tall he is and i don't know how much he weighs he has black hair and a moustache he is a car dealer in riyadh saudi arabia he sells mercedes benz and porsche cars his company is large more than 50 people work for him my father is very smart i love my father but i don't see him a lot usually he is at his company or with my brothers i think that he is the best father in the world to his fifteen children

Now edit your paragraph. If necessary, make changes in grammar, punctuation, and any other item, and then give the edited paragraph to your teacher.

Expanding

Imagine that one of these men is your father. Write a paragraph about him. Include his name, job, personality, likes/dislikes, and other items. Your paragraph can be serious or funny.

Paragraph 3

Write about your classmate.

This woman is Ursula Kaaris. Look at her picture. What do you think about her? Does she look like a friendly person? How tall do you think she is? Do you think you would like to know her?

Prewriting

A classmate of Ursula Kaaris wrote this paragraph. How does the writer describe Ursula's face? Does the writer describe her face from bottom to top or top to bottom? Are there any parts of her face not described?

My classmate is Ursula Kaaris. She is 18 years old, and she is from Hillerod, Denmark. Her face is oblong. Her hair is long and brown. Her ears are small. Her eyebrows are medium, and her eyelashes are long. Her eyes are gray. Her nose is not short and not long. Her cheeks are full and smooth. Her mouth is wide, and her lips are thin. She is wearing an unusual pale violet-colored lipstick that matches her pale violet fingernails. In Denmark, Ursula is a university student. She doesn't know what job she wants in the future. She wants to travel a lot in the United States.

The following cluster was made by the writer. Notice the information the writer uses. What are five items the writer does not use? Why not?

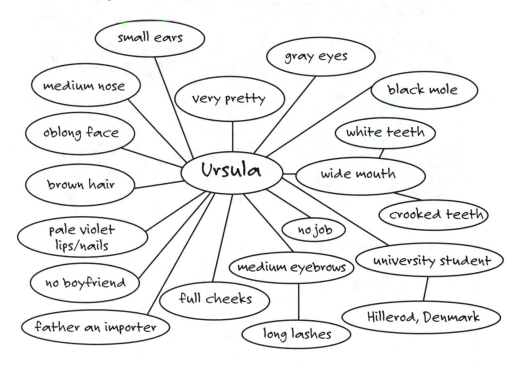

Think about vocabulary. The writer describes specific parts of the face. Match the following:

1. ___	the hair above a man's lip	A. cheek
2. ___	the space between the eyes and the hairline on top of the head	B. eyebrow
3. ___	small hairs attached to the eyelids	C. wrinkles
4. ___	lines in a person's face	D. moustache
5. ___	the bottom of the face	E. forehead
6. ___	the hair above each eye	F. eyelashes
7. ___	the part of the face under each eye and beside the nose on both sides	G. chin

Talk to a classmate. Find out about the person. Use these questions to guide you. How would you describe:

the shape of your head?   your forehead?
your hair?   your eyebrows?
your eyelashes?   your eyes?
your cheeks?   your nose?
your mouth?   your lips?
your chin?

What is the most unusual feature on your face?
What is your job in your country?
What kind of job do you want in the future?
What are two things you want to do in the future?
Write your notes below.

_____

_____

_____

_____

_____

_____

Think about your conversation. Is there any other important information you want to add? Make a cluster about your classmate.

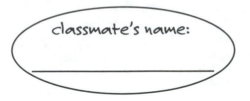

classmate's name:
_____

Writing

Use the cluster to write a paragraph about your classmate. Again, you don't have to use all of the cluster, and you may add information not in the cluster. Don't worry about grammar here.

_____

_____

_____

_____

_____

_____

_____

_____

_____

_____

_____

_____

Sharing

Ask your classmate (the person you described) to read your paragraph and tell you what he or she likes or doesn't like. What do you think should be changed?

Revising

Rewrite your paragraph. Change whatever you want. Try to give a clear picture of your classmate.

_____

_____

_____

_____

_____

_____

_____

_____

_____

_____

_____

_____

_____

_____

Editing

Complete the following exercises.

Exercise A:　Using verbs and pronouns

　　Directions:　Fill in each space using **is, are, he, his,** or **my.**

　　_____ classmate is Ernesto Lopez. He _____ 22 years
　　　　　1　　　　　　　　　　　　　　　　　　　2

old. _____ is from Buenos Aires, Argentina. Ernesto _____
　　　3　　　　　　　　　　　　　　　　　　　　　　　　　4

a winemaker in Buenos Aires. _____ wants to study
　　　　　　　　　　　　　　　　5

winemaking at an American university. _____ face _____
　　　　　　　　　　　　　　　　　　　　6　　　　　　7

round. His hair _____ medium length and blond. _____
　　　　　　　　　　8　　　　　　　　　　　　　　　　　　9

ears _____ small. His eyebrows _____ thick. _____ eyes
　　　　10　　　　　　　　　　　　　　11　　　　　　12

are green. His nose _____ long. _____ cheeks _____ red
　　　　　　　　　　　13　　　　　　14　　　　　　15

and rough. _____ mouth _____ small. Ernesto _____ a
　　　　　　　16　　　　　　17　　　　　　　　　18

very friendly person.

Exercise B: Forming compound sentences.

Directions: A **comma** and a **coordinate conjunction** can join two sentences. Form a single compound sentence from each pair of simple sentences.

Example: She is 18 years old. She is from Hillerod, Denmark. She is 18 years old, **and** she is from Hillerod, Denmark.

1. Her face is oblong. Her hair is long.

   _____

   _____

2. Ernesto is a winemaker. He wants to study winemaking at an American university.

   _____

   _____

3. Her eyelashes are long. Her eyes are gray.

   _____

   _____

4. She is 22 years old. She is majoring in chemistry.

   _____

   _____

5. His eyebrows are thick. His eyes are green.

   _____

   _____

Exercise C: Writing compound sentences

Directions: Fill in the blanks to make compound sentences. Use your imagination.

1. Her eyes are happy, and _____.
2. His hair is black, but _____.
3. She loves to play basketball, but _____.
4. He likes to kiss girls, and _____.
5. She likes to walk her dog, and _____.
6. Susan's nose is small _____.
7. José studies physics _____.
8. Sook-kyoung likes to go to the beach _____.
9. David enjoys eating Chinese food _____.
10. Mika watches television a lot _____.

Go back and check your paragraphs. Did you use compound sentences? Find two places where you can make compound sentences.

Exercise D: Using adjectives and nouns

> *Directions:* Fill in the blanks with any adjective or noun.
> Use your imagination.

One of my friends in this class is Anabel Tatis. She is a young _____. She is from _____. Her face is
_____. Her hair is _____ and _____. Her
ears are _____. Her eyebrows are _____ and
_____. Her mouth is _____. Today Anabel is
wearing a _____ skirt and a _____ blouse. Her
_____ are _____. Anabel is a _____ in her
country. She wants to study _____ in the United States.
After her studies, she wants to travel to _____ and
_____, and _____. In her free time, Anabel likes
to play _____ and _____. She is a very
_____ person.

Now edit your paragraph and it give it to your teacher.

Expanding

Imagine that you will live on a tropical island for the rest of your life with one other person. You cannot choose a real person. Create the person you want to live with. Describe the person's looks, personality, and interests.

Paragraph

4

Write about the place where you live.

Look at this picture of a living room. Does it look like the living room where you live? How is it similar? How is it different?

Prewriting

Hiroyuki Osada wrote this paragraph about the place where he lives. Read his paragraph silently. Write down four reasons you would not like to live in his apartment.

My American roommate and I have a simple apartment at 237 Cranbrook Court. It is a medium-sized apartment. It has a kitchen, living room, bedroom, and bathroom. In the kitchen, there are an old wooden table, four new metal and plastic chairs, an electric stove, a small General Electric refrigerator, and lots of dirty dishes in the sink. Sometimes, at night, we have mice and bugs on the floor. The living room has a brown vinyl sofa with lots of holes in it, one table with a broken lamp, and one big green chair. Old pictures of Michael Jordan and Madonna are on the wall. The bedroom has two beds, two desks, two lamps, a small chest of drawers, and piles of dirty clothes. The bathroom has a dirty toilet, bathtub, sink, and mirror. The shower doesn't work. Our apartment is OK, but it is not fantastic.

Reason 1 _____

Reason 2 _____

Reason 3 _____

Reason 4 _____

Hiroyuki's paragraph has many specific details such as *237 Cranbrook Court*, a small *General Electric* refrigerator, a *brown vinyl* sofa, old pictures of *Michael Jordan* and *Madonna*. Make the following details more specific:

1. in the _____ kitchen   5. on the _____ wall

2. a _____ electric stove   6. two _____ beds

3. _____ mice and bugs   7. one _____ table

4. the _____ bathroom

Think about vocabulary. Look at the following household items. List each one in the room where it belongs. Some items may be in more than one room. What other household items can you think of?

dishwasher	dresser	bookcase
mattress	microwave	carpet
refrigerator	toilet paper	closet
sink	chest of drawers	cupboard
pillows	couch	desk

BEDROOM	**BATHROOM**	**LIVING ROOM**	**KITCHEN**
_____	_____	_____	_____
_____	_____	_____	_____
_____	_____	_____	_____
_____	_____	_____	_____
_____	_____	_____	_____
_____	_____	_____	_____
_____	_____	_____	_____

Talk to a classmate. Discuss the place where you live. Use these questions to guide you.

1. What is your address?
2. Is it a house, apartment, dorm room, or something else?
3. How many rooms does it have?
4. Describe five items that are in each room.
5. What do you like about the place?
6. What do you not like about the place?

Write your notes below.

_____

_____

_____

Think about your conversation. Is there anything you left out? Make a cluster about the place where you live.

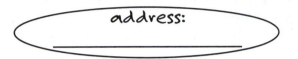

address:

_____

Writing

Now give your cluster to one of your classmates. Write a paragraph using *another person's* cluster. Feel free to make changes as you write.

_____

_____

_____

_____

_____

_____

_____

_____

_____

_____

_____

_____

_____

Sharing

Give your paragraph to the person whose cluster you were using. Now look at the paragraph that is about the place where you live. Is it a good description? Is the information communicated clearly?

Revising

Rewrite your classmate's paragraph about the place where you live. You may change words, phrases, sentences, or the whole paragraph.

_____

_____

_____

_____

_____

_____

_____

_____

_____

_____

_____

_____

_____

_____

Editing

Complete the following exercises.

Exercise A: Using verbs

Directions: Fill in each space with **is, are, have,** or **has.**

My Chinese friend and I _____ an apartment on Russell
                              1
Street. It _____ a very small apartment. It _____ a
              2   3
kitchen/living room, bedroom, and bathroom. The kitchen
_____ a plastic table, two chairs, a gas stove, and a small
    4
refrigerator. We _____ an old Zenith TV and some cushions
                     5
in the living room. There _____ four pictures on the wall: a
                              6
white kitten, yellow flowers, a girl with a violin, and a reprint
of a Van Gogh. The bedroom _____ two beds, two desks,
                              7
and two lamps. There _____ one dresser for our clothes. The
                         8
bathroom _____ a toilet, shower, sink, and mirror. Our
            9
apartment _____ always clean because my roommate is
              10
crazy about cleaning.

Exercise B: Using punctuation and capitalization

Directions: Names of apartment buildings and streets start with **capital letters**. Items in series have a **comma** between them. Edit the paragraph by adding periods, capitals, and commas.

Example: It has a kitchen , living room , and bedroom.

    my american roommate and i have a simple apartment at 237 cranbrook court it is a medium-sized apartment it has a kitchen living room bedroom and bathroom in the kitchen there are an old wooden table four new metal and plastic chairs an electric stove a small general electric refrigerator and lots of dirty dishes in the sink sometimes at night we have mice and bugs on the kitchen floor the living room has a brown vinyl sofa with lots of holes in it one table with a broken lamp and one big green chair pictures of michael jordan and madonna are on the wall the bedroom has two desks two lamps a small chest of drawers two beds and piles of dirty clothes the bathroom has a toilet bathtub sink and mirror the shower doesn't work our apartment is OK but it is not fantastic

Now edit your paragraph. Go back and check the verbs, punctuation, and capitalization in your paragraphs. Make any necessary changes and submit it to your teacher.

Expanding

Work with two of your classmates. Imagine that you want to build a new apartment or house. Design three rooms (one person design the kitchen, one person design the living area, one person design the bedroom/bathroom area). Draw pictures of the rooms and compare them with those of other groups.

Write about your home city and its people.

The city in the photographs is Rome. What do you know about Rome? Have you ever visited there? What is in Rome? Do you know any Italians?

Prewriting

Read the following paragraphs about Rome. Then discuss both paragraphs with your class. Which one gives you more information about Rome? Fill in the outline with your class.

I am from Rome. Rome is in Italy, and it is the magnificent capital of Italy. It is a very large city. It has many people. Rome usually has nice weather because it is close to the sea. Rome also has many famous fantastic things to see. Rome also has many beautiful parks. Romans like to walk in the parks, and we like to sit in the comfortable cafés. We like to watch people, and we are always in love. Every Roman likes to have fun, and Rome is a great city to have fun in!

I am from Rome. Rome is in southern Italy, and it is the magnificent capital of Italy. It is a very large city. It has about three million people. Rome usually has warm weather because it is close to the Mediterranean Sea. Rome also has many fantastic things to see. For example, the Vatican, the Colosseum, and the Fountain of Trevi are in Rome. Rome also has many beautiful parks. Romans like to walk in the parks, and we like to sit in the comfortable cafés. We like to watch people, and we are always in love. Every Roman likes to have fun, and Rome is a great city to have fun in!

Outline

City _____

  I. Geographical location _____

_____

  II. Population _____

_____

  III. Climate _____

_____

  IV. Things to see _____

_____

_____

_____

_____

_____

  V. What Romans do _____

_____

_____

_____

_____

_____

Think about vocabulary. As you describe your city and its people, you will need to use adjectives. Look in the second paragraph and find eight adjectives:

_____   _____

_____   _____

_____   _____

_____   _____

Think of an adjective to put into the following blanks. You may use a dictionary if necessary:

the _____ Mediterranean Sea

the _____ Coliseum

the _____ Fountain of Trevi

in the _____ parks

like to watch _____ people

Talk to two of your classmates. Interview them about their native cities. Be sure to find out each city's location, population, weather, history, interesting sites (at least three), nightlife, kinds of people, and bad points. Ask any other question you want. Your conversation with each student should last about ten minutes.

Make a cluster about your native city. Be sure to include some of its good points and bad points.

native city:

_____

Writing

Write a paragraph using your cluster. Be relaxed, and concentrate on your ideas.

_____

_____

_____

_____

_____

_____

_____

_____

_____

_____

_____

_____

Sharing

Ask one of your classmates to read your paragraph to you. What do you think? Can you understand everything you have written? Does the reader understand your ideas?

Revising

Revise your paragraph. Continue to concentrate on ideas. Think about the order of your ideas. Put the most important point last.

_____

_____

_____

_____

_____

_____

_____

_____

_____

_____

_____

_____

_____

Editing

Think about your paragraph as you do the following exercises.

Exercise A: Using verbs

> *Directions:* Fill in the spaces with **am, is, are, has, have,** or **like.**

I _____ from Shagra. Shagra _____ in central Jordan.
    1   2

Shagra _____ a medium-sized city; it _____ about 30,000
          3   4

people. The weather _____ very hot in Shagra because it
                        5

_____ in the desert. The temperature _____ usually
  6   7

42–46°C in the summer. Nothing famous _____ in Shagra.
                                8

My town _____ many markets, shops, and stores, but no
         9

large buildings _____ in Shagra. The people of Shagra
            10

_____ to sit in the cafés, go to the mosques, and visit their
  11

friends' houses. Shagra _____ a normal city, and I _____
                  12   13

many friends there.

Exercise B: Using compound sentences

> *Directions:* Join each pair of sentences to make one compound sentence.

1. Romans like to walk in the parks. (**and**) We like to sit in the cafés.

   _____

   _____

2. We like to watch people. (**and**) We are always in love.

   _____

   _____

3. My town has many markets. (**but**) No large buildings are there.

   _____

   _____

4. It is a very large city. (**and**) It has about three million lovely people.

   _____

   _____

Exercise C: Writing compound sentences

> *Directions:* Write down three compound sentences from your paragraph.

1. _____

   _____

   _____

2. _____

   _____

   _____

3. _____

   _____

   _____

Exercise D: Using articles

> *Directions:* Use *the* before the specific names of seas, oceans, and buildings. Fill in the space with **a, an,** or **the,** or leave the space blank.

1. I am from _____ Rome.

2. Rome is in _____ southern Italy, and it is _____ capital of Italy.

3. It is_____ very large city.

4. It has about _____ three million people.

5. _____ Rome usually has warm weather because it is close to _____ Mediterranean Sea.

6. _____ Rome also has many famous things to see.

7. For example, _____ Vatican, _____ Colosseum, and _____ Fountain of Trevi are in _____ Rome.

8. Romans like to walk in _____ parks, and we like to sit in _____ cafés.

9. _____ Rome is _____ great city to have fun in.

When you finish, edit your paragraph and give it to your teacher.

Expanding

As a class project, produce a booklet about the city, town, or neighborhood where you are. Work in teams. Your teacher will assign one topic about your city, town, or neighborhood to each team. (For example, restaurants, banks, coffee houses, parks, hair salons, museums, etc.) Your team's goal is to get information about your topic. Choose the best and the worst examples of each topic. Gather each team's information together in booklet form. Make copies for each class member.

Write about what your classmate's mother does every day.

Look at the pictures. Which one of the women reminds you more of your mother? Why? Which reminds you less? Why? When the word "mother" comes to mind, what qualities do you think of?

Prewriting

Read the following paragraph silently. When you finish, do the exercise with one of your classmates.

Rachel's mother, Ruth, has a busy and interesting life. Ruth usually wakes up at 6:30 A.M. Then she likes to lie in bed for a while and drink coffee. After about half an hour, she likes to get up and go to work on the trees and flowers around the apartment. At about 8:00 she goes back inside and takes a shower. Then she dresses, and goes to exercise with her friends. When she finishes her exercises, she goes shopping. She comes home at around 10:30, cleans the house, and cooks some lunch. From 12:00 to 12:30, she eats lunch with her husband, Shuka. From then until 7:30, she teaches piano, organ, and accordion to her students. When she finishes, she eats dinner with her husband. In the evening she likes to play cards or go dancing. At about 11:30, she and her husband usually go to sleep.

Look at the following schedule of Rachel's mother's activities. What are five instances in which the schedule disagrees with the information in the paragraph?

6:30 A.M.	wakes up
6:30–7:00	lies in bed/drinks coffee
7:00–8:00	gets dressed, works on flowers
8:00–10:30	takes a shower, finishes exercises, goes shopping
11:00–12:00	comes home/cleans/cooks
12:00–12:30 P.M.	eats lunch with her husband
1:00–7:30	teaches piano, organ, and accordion
7:30	goes dancing
11:00	goes to sleep

Think about vocabulary. Notice how prepositional phrases of time are used in the paragraph. Discuss with your class what each means. Practice using them with your teacher:

at 6:30 A.M.	at around 10:30
for a while	from 12:00 to 12:30
about half an hour	from then until 7:30
at about 8:00	in the evening

Talk to your classmate. Ask about her or his mother (or spouse or child). Write down, in schedule form, at least eight things the person does every day.

Schedule

_____

_____

_____

_____

_____

_____

_____

_____

_____

_____

_____

_____

_____

Writing

Use the schedule to write a paragraph about your classmate's mother (or spouse or child).

_____

_____

_____

_____

_____

_____

_____

_____

_____

_____

_____

_____

_____

_____

Sharing

Show your paragraph to your classmate. Ask your classmate to make at least *three* changes in the paragraph (add, reorder, subtract).

Revising

Revise the paragraph using changes your classmate suggested.

_____

_____

_____

_____

_____

_____

_____

_____

_____

_____

_____

_____

_____

_____

Editing

Think about your paragraph as you do these exercises.

Exercise A: Using verbs

> *Directions:* Choose the appropriate verb. Make it
> **third person singular.**

go (2)	clean	read	leave
make (2)	eat	watch	get
come	take	sew	

Her mother, Hisae, _____ up at 6:00 A.M. every day.
               1

From 6:00 to 7:00 A.M., she _____ breakfast for the
                       2

family. At 7:00 A.M. she _____ the house and _____
                 3   4

shopping. She _____ back at 10:00 A.M. and _____
           5   6

the house. She _____ lunch by herself at 12:30 P.M. In the
           7

afternoon, she usually _____ a nap from 2:00 to 4:00 P.M.
               8

From 4:00 to 6:00 P.M., she _____ her favorite TV
                 9

programs. At 6:00 P.M. she _____ dinner for the family.
              10

After dinner, she _____ novels and _____. She
           11   12

_____ to sleep with her husband at about 10:30 P.M.
   13

Exercise B: Using punctuation and capitalization

Directions: Add capital letters, periods, and commas.

rachel's mother ruth has a busy and interesting life ruth usually wakes up at 6:30 A.M. then she likes to lie in bed for a while and drink coffee after about half an hour she likes to get up and go to work on the trees and flowers around the apartment at about 8:00 she goes back inside and takes a shower then she dresses and she goes to exercise with her friends when she finishes her exercises she goes shopping she comes home at around 10:30 cleans the house and cooks some lunch from 12:00 to 12:30 she eats lunch with her husband shuka from then until 7:30 she teaches piano organ and accordion to her students when she finishes she eats dinner with her husband in the evening she likes to play cards or go dancing at about 11:30 she and her husband usually go to sleep

Exercise C: Using prepositions of time

Directions: Fill in the spaces with **at, from...to,** or **in.**

1. She usually wakes up _____ 6:30 A.M.

2. _____ 6:30 _____ 7:00 she lies in bed and drinks coffee.

3. _____ 7:00 she likes to get up and go to work on the flowers around the house.

4. She comes home _____ 10:30, cleans the house, and cooks some lunch.

5. _____ 12:00 _____ 12:30, she eats lunch with her husband.

6. _____ the evening she likes to play cards or go dancing.

7. _____ 11:30 she and her husband go to sleep.

Exercise D: Creating proper sentence order

Directions: These sentences are not in the right order. Copy them in the right order in paragraph form below.

She comes back at 10:00 A.M. and cleans the house. From 4:00 to 6:00 P.M., she watches her favorite TV programs. She goes to sleep with her husband at about 10:30 P.M. She eats her lunch by herself at 12:30 P.M. Her mother, Hisae, gets up at 6:00 A.M. every day. After dinner she reads novels and sews. In the afternoon, she usually takes a nap from 2:00 to 4:00 P.M. From 6:00 to 7:00 A.M. she makes breakfast for the family. At 7:00 A.M. she leaves the house and goes shopping. At 6:00 P.M. she makes dinner for the family.

_____

_____

_____

_____

_____

_____

_____

_____

_____

_____

_____

_____

_____

Now edit your paragraph and submit it.

Expanding

Have some discussion fun with your class. Get up and walk around your class asking people questions about their everyday schedule and activities.

List the names of two people in your class who usually:

wake up before 6 A.M.   _____   _____

don't eat breakfast.   _____   _____

drink over two cups of morning coffee.   _____   _____

exercise in the morning.   _____   _____

have a sandwich or hamburger for lunch. _____   _____

listen to music in the afternoon.   _____   _____

read a book in the afternoon.   _____   _____

play a sport during the day.   _____   _____

walk more than 2 miles a day.   _____   _____

drive more than 20 miles a day.   _____   _____

smoke a cigarette.   _____   _____

have an alcoholic drink.   _____   _____

eat dinner between 7 and 8 P.M.   _____   _____

cook dinner.   _____   _____

go out to a restaurant for dinner.   _____   _____

kiss someone.   _____   _____

do homework after 9 P.M.   _____   _____

watch TV after 10 P.M.   _____   _____

go to sleep after 12 A.M.   _____   _____

Write about what you are doing right now.

What are the people in the picture doing? Point out different activities that are taking place in the picture.

Prewriting

Read the following paragraph aloud with your class. Then discuss the questions after the paragraph.

I am sitting on the wet grass outside our English classroom. There is a lot of trash on the ground. I am sitting under a big oak tree. The sun is not shining. Big, black clouds are moving across the sky. The wind is blowing hard. Some cups are blowing across the lawn. A crow is flying in the wind. I see many people. Some are walking to their classes. Some are going to the library. Only our class is sitting on the grass. Two guys are slowly riding by on their bicycles. I think they are talking and laughing, but I can't hear them. They are wearing heavy coats. I am wearing only a thin sweater. Because it is cold, I am stopping.

Questions

1. What season of the year do you think it is?

   _____

2. What kind of trash do you think is on the ground?

   _____

3. What change in weather do you think is about to happen?

   _____

4. Why are the guys riding slowly?

   _____

5. Why can't the writer hear the guys?

   _____

6. Why do you think the grass is wet?

   _____

7. Why do you think the class is sitting outside on the wet grass?

   _____

Think about vocabulary. Use a dictionary if necessary. Replace the following words with synonyms:

1. There is _____ _____ on the ground.
   <u>a lot of</u>   <u>trash</u>

2. I am sitting under a _____ oak tree.
                       <u>big</u>

3. _____ black clouds are _____ across the sky.
      <u>Big</u>   <u>moving</u>

4. The wind is blowing _____.
                      <u>hard</u>

5. A crow is _____ in the wind.
              <u>flying</u>

6. Some are _____ to their classes.
              <u>walking</u>

7. Some are _____ to the library.
              <u>going</u>

8. I _____ they are talking and laughing, but I can't hear them.
       <u>think</u>

If it isn't too cold or wet, go outside with your class and find a comfortable place to sit. Make a cluster of the things you feel, hear, and see all around you as you sit.

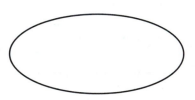

Writing

Use the cluster to write a paragraph about what you felt, heard, and saw. Write as if these things are happening right now.

_____

_____

_____

_____

_____

_____

_____

_____

_____

_____

_____

_____

_____

_____

Sharing

Read your paragraph to a small group of your classmates. Ask them what they think. Do they understand everything? Did you communicate your feelings and observations well? After your classmates give their opinions, read your paragraph again. Is there anything you want to change?

Revising

Rewrite your paragraph. Change whatever you want. Work especially hard on improving your vocabulary.

_____

_____

_____

_____

_____

_____

_____

_____

_____

_____

_____

_____

_____

_____

Editing

Complete the following exercises. Then edit your paragraph and submit it to your teacher.

Exercise A: Using verbs

Directions: Fill in the right form of the **present continuous.**

I (sit) _____ in Shields Library on the University of
         1

California, Davis campus. I (sit) _____ at a large brown
                                     2

table with two students. They (study) _____
                                          3

mathematics. They (talk) _____ very quietly. Several
                             4

students (look) _____ for books in the stacks. One
                    5

student (drink) _____ water from a water fountain. He
                    6

(hit) _____ himself in the eye with the water. One boy
        7

at another table (scratch) _____ his head with his
                               8

pencil. The air conditioner (blow) _____ cold air at me.
                                       9

I (move) _____ because I don't want to get sick.
             10

Exercise B: Using prepositions of space and direction

Directions: Fill in the blanks with **on, under, across, in**, or **to**.

1. I am sitting _____ the wet grass.

2. I am sitting _____ a big tree.

3. Big, black clouds are moving _____ the sky.

4. A bird is flying _____ the wind.

5. Some students are walking _____ their classes.

6. Some are going _____ the library.

7. Our class is sitting _____ the grass.

8. Two guys are slowly riding by _____ their bicycles.

Expanding

Read the following poem.

    Students in a park

    A picnic and barbecue

    I wish I was there!

Use your imagination. Write a poem about some thing(s) you see now.

_____

_____

_____

_____

_____

_____

_____

Write about your best or worst former teacher.

Look at the picture. What seems to be the relationship between the teacher and the student? Is it this way in your country? What is a typical classroom like in your country?

Prewriting

Read and discuss the following paragraph about Mr. Kenji Aoki. The paragraph was written by Shige Matsunori. What does Shige think about Mr. Aoki? What do you think about him?

My favorite teacher was Mr. Kenji Aoki. He was a small, old man with gray hair and a gray beard. He was my fifth-grade mathematics teacher in Osaka, Japan. Mr. Aoki was hard, but friendly. For me, mathematics was a terrible subject. Many of my classmates were very good in math, but I was not. I had many problems, but Mr. Aoki was usually ready to help me, especially after class. His class was very difficult. We had a test every two days. Every night there were at least fifteen pages of homework. Many nights I was sick of math, but the homework was important. I was sorry at the end of the year. Mr. Aoki was a good teacher, and he helped me a lot.

Fill in the empty places in the cluster that Shige made.

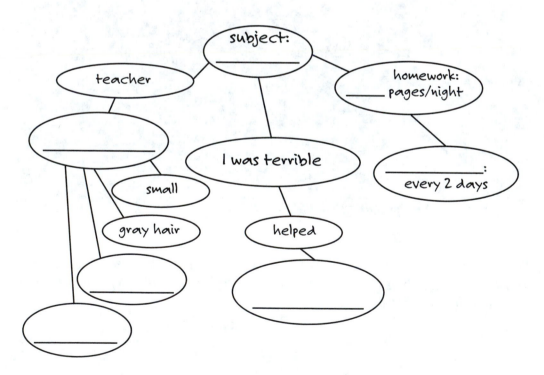

Think about vocabulary. Work with a partner. Write down the opposite of each of these words from the paragraph:

1. favorite: _____
2. small: _____
3. old: _____
4. hard: _____
5. friendly: _____
6. terrible: _____
7. many: _____
8. good: _____

9. ready: _____
10. after: _____
11. difficult: _____
12. important: _____
13. sorry: _____
14. end: _____
15. a lot: _____

Talk with a classmate. Discuss a memorable teacher. Use these questions to guide you:

Who was your best (or worst) teacher?

What subject did she/he teach you?

What school were you in?

Why was the teacher so good (or bad)?

Describe the typical classroom of this teacher.

_____

_____

_____

Give three specific examples of times when this teacher helped (or didn't help) you.

_____

_____

_____

Make a cluster about the teacher. Remember what you talked about with your classmate. Include other details.

name:

_____

Writing

Write a paragraph based on your cluster. Try hard to make your classmates understand why you remember the teacher so well.

_____

_____

_____

_____

_____

_____

_____

_____

_____

_____

_____

_____

_____

Sharing

Exchange your cluster from the Prewriting section for that of a classmate. On a separate piece of paper write a paragraph based on your classmate's cluster, while he or she writes a paragraph based on yours. When you finish, trade paragraphs with your classmate. Compare your classmate's paragraph with your paragraph in the Writing section. Both paragraphs are based on the same cluster. How are they different?

Revising

Rewrite the paragraph you wrote in the Writing section. You may use some of your classmate's words or sentences if you want.

_____

_____

_____

_____

_____

_____

_____

_____

_____

_____

_____

_____

_____

Editing

Before you edit your paragraph, complete the following exercises.

Exercise A: Using verbs

Directions: Fill in the spaces with **was** or **were**.

My best teacher _____ Ms. Sylvie Goncourt. She
$\underset{1}{}$

_____ a young woman with brown hair and glasses. She
$\underset{2}{}$

_____ my eighth-grade French teacher in Antwerp, Belgium.
$\underset{3}{}$

Ms. Goncourt's explanations _____ clear and interesting.
$\underset{4}{}$

She _____ close to her students. French _____ an easy
$\underset{5}{}$ $\underset{6}{}$

subject for me in general, but some things _____ difficult,
$\underset{7}{}$

such as grammar and composition. Ms. Goncourt _____
$\underset{8}{}$

able to explain the most difficult points very easily and clearly.

Also, most of her classes _____ very interesting because
$\underset{9}{}$

there _____ something new every day. I _____ lucky to
$\underset{10}{}$ $\underset{11}{}$

have Ms. Sylvie Goncourt as my teacher.

Exercise B: Using punctuation and capitalization

> *Directions:* Add **periods, capitals,** and **commas**. Names of cities and countries should be separated by commas.

my favorite teacher was mr kenji aoki he was a small old man with gray hair and a gray beard he was my fifth-grade mathematics teacher in osaka japan mr aoki was hard but friendly for me mathematics was a terrible subject many of my classmates were very good in math but i was not i had many problems but mr aoki was usually ready to help me especially after class his class was very difficult we had a test every two days every night there were at least fifteen pages of homework many nights i was sick of math but the homework was important i was sorry at the end of the year mr aoki was a good teacher and he helped me a lot

Exercise C: Recognizing compound sentences

> *Directions:* Write down all of the compound sentences that you see in the paragraphs about Mr. Aoki and Ms. Goncourt.

_____

_____

_____

_____

_____

_____

_____

_____

Exercise D: Using pronouns

Directions: Change the names in boldface type to **she, he, her,** or **his.**

Example: **Ms. Sylvie Goncourt** (*She*) was a young woman with brown hair and glasses.

1. **Ms. Goncourt** (   ) was my eighth-grade French teacher.

2. I had many problems, but **Mr. Aoki** (   ) was always ready to help me.

3. **Mr. Aoki's** (   ) class was very difficult.

4. Most of **Ms. Goncourt's** (   ) classes were very interesting.

5. I was lucky to have **Ms. Sylvie Goncourt** (   ) as my teacher.

6. **Mr. Aoki** (   ) was a good teacher, and he helped me a lot.

Expanding

Study the pictures. Choose the classroom you like best. Imagine that you were in the class last month. Write a paragraph about the class. Tell about the teacher, the subject you were taking, what you did in class every day, how much homework you had, and other things that you think were important.

Paragraph

9

Write about what you did last weekend, or on a recent trip.

Look at the picture. What types of trips do you like to take? Do you prefer the mountains? The beach? A forest? What do you like to do on short trips?

Prewriting

Read and discuss the following paragraph with your class. Complete the organizational diagram by yourself, then compare your answers with those of your classmates.

Last Sunday, my friends and I went to San Francisco. We visited Golden Gate Park, Chinatown, and Fisherman's Wharf. At 10:00 in the morning we went to the Steinhart Aquarium in the park. We saw many different kinds of sharks, fish, and crazy people. After two hours, we drove to Chinatown. We ate lunch there. We had almond chicken, mushi pork, and steamed rice. I got a fortune cookie that said "You will inherit a million dollars." At about 2:00 we took an exciting ride in a cable car to Fisherman's Wharf. While we were there, we took a boat ride around the bay, we shopped at Pier 39 and the Cannery, and we all drank milkshakes at an ice cream store at Ghirardelli Square. When we went back to our car at 5:00, we found a $25.00 ticket on the windshield.

Golden Gate Park _____ _____

_____ crazy people

_____ lunch _____

_____

_____

city

fortune cookie

_____ _____

_____ Pier 39

_____

Ghirardelli Square

Think about vocabulary. There are 20 words from the paragraph in the following square. How many of them can you find?

San Francisco	square	Chinatown	milkshake
chicken	rice	fortune	cookie
windshield	shark	million	ride
park	aquarium	inherit	crazy
fish	boat	car	ice

S	A	N	F	R	A	N	C	I	S	C	O
Q	K	H	O	K	R	A	H	S	E	H	Z
U	H	S	R	M	Y	Q	I	T	I	I	M
A	I	I	T	I	Z	C	C	I	K	N	U
R	C	F	U	P	A	R	K	R	O	A	I
E	E	I	N	R	R	E	E	E	O	T	R
T	E	S	E	A	C	I	N	H	C	O	A
A	D	L	E	I	H	S	D	N	I	W	U
O	I	B	A	M	I	L	L	I	O	N	Q
B	R	E	K	A	H	S	K	L	I	M	A

Talk with three classmates. Take turns describing your weekend. As each person finishes, the other three classmates must each ask two questions about what the person described.

Think about what you did last weekend, or remember a trip you took. Make a cluster of your experiences.

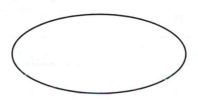

Writing

Write a paragraph based on your cluster. Try to include as many examples as possible.

_____

_____

_____

_____

_____

_____

_____

_____

_____

_____

_____

_____

_____

Sharing

Give your paragraph to a classmate. Ask your classmate to draw a diagram of your paragraph similar to the one on page 77 while you draw a diagram of your classmate's paragraph.

Revising

Look at the diagram that your classmate drew. Did your classmate understand your ideas and organization? Rewrite your paragraph, making any changes you think are necessary.

_____

_____

_____

_____

_____

_____

_____

_____

_____

_____

_____

_____

_____

_____

Editing

Think about your paragraph as you complete the following exercises. Then edit your paragraph and submit it to your teacher.

Exercise A: Using complex sentences.

Directions: A **complex sentence** is a sentence with at least one dependent clause and one independent clause. A dependent clause contains a subordinator + subject + verb. An independent clause contains subject + verb (no subordinator). Change each of the following to a complex sentence.

Example: (**After**) We visited Underground Atlanta. We went to a baseball game.

<u>After we visited Underground Atlanta</u>, <u>we went to a baseball game.</u>
       dependent clause   independent clause

1. (**While**) We were in Atlanta. We visited Underground Atlanta, Peachtree Street, and Stone Mountain.

   _____

   _____

2. (**After**) We stayed in Underground Atlanta for two hours. We shopped on Peachtree Street.

   _____

   _____

3. We finished shopping. (**Before**) We went to Stone Mountain.

   _____

   _____

4. We took a bus. (**When**) We went to Stone Mountain.

   _____

   _____

5. (**While**) We were at Stone Mountain. We rode a train.

   _____

   _____

Exercise B: Writing complex sentences.

Directions: Write five complex sentences about any subject.

1. _____

   _____

2. _____

   _____

3. _____

   _____

4. _____

   _____

5. _____

   _____

Exercise C: Using prepositions

Directions: Fill in the spaces with **at, around, to, of,** or **in.**

Last Sunday, my friends and I went _____ San
                                              1
Francisco. _____ 10:00 in the morning we went _____
              2   3
the Steinhart Aquarium _____ the park. We saw many
                            4
different kinds _____ sharks and fish. After two hours, we
                     5
drove _____ Chinatown. _____ about 2:00 we took a
         6   7
cable car _____ Fisherman's Wharf. We took a boat ride
              8
_____ the bay, and we shopped _____ Pier 39 and the
    9   10
Cannery. We all drank milkshakes _____ an ice cream store
                                      11
_____ Ghirardelli Square.
    12

Expanding

Write a paragraph about one city in the United States you would like to visit. Be sure to include many specific details.

_____

_____

_____

_____

_____

_____

_____

_____

_____

_____

_____

_____

_____

_____

_____

_____

_____

_____

Paragraph

10

Write about your classmate's best childhood friend.

Look at the pictures. Do you have many friends? Who is your best friend? How long have you known your best friend? Where is your best friend now?

Prewriting

Read and discuss the following paragraph with your class. Make a list of ten things you do *not* know about Masoume Abbas. Would the paragraph be better with some of these things included?

My classmate is Fatima Sharadi of Tehran, Iran. When she was a child, her best friend was Masoume Abbas. Fatima and Masoume went to kindergarten and elementary school together in Tehran. They also had the same piano teacher. They did many things together. They played games in the park, sang songs, and did their homework together. Sometimes their families went on vacation to the Caspian Sea together. One time they had a fight that lasted two years, but they became friends again. After elementary school, they went to different middle schools, high schools, and universities. Today they still write letters and make telephone calls to each other.

1. _____
2. _____
3. _____
4. _____
5. _____
6. _____
7. _____
8. _____
9. _____
10. _____

Think about vocabulary. Notice the way that the writer of the paragraph introduces new time elements:

When she was a child,
One time they had a fight
After elementary school,
Today they still write letters

Which one of the above is a dependent clause?

Look at some other words you can use to begin dependent time clauses:

before   whenever   as soon as   since

Practice making complex sentences with them.

Talk to your classmate. Discuss her/his best childhood friend. Use these questions to guide you:

What was your friend's name?
How long have you known your friend?
How did you first meet your friend? How old were you?
Please describe your friend.
What were some of the things you did together?
What was the funniest time you ever had together?
Did you ever get in trouble?
Are you still friends today?

_____

_____

_____

_____

_____

Writing

Use the answers to write a paragraph. Remember to focus on ideas.

_____

_____

_____

_____

_____

_____

_____

_____

_____

_____

_____

_____

_____

_____

_____

_____

Sharing

Give your paragraph to the classmate you interviewed. Read the paragraph based on the interview with you. What do you think? How could the paragraph about your childhood friend be better?

Revising

Rewrite the paragraph about your own childhood friend. You can take sentences out, add sentences, or reorder sentences.

_____

_____

_____

_____

_____

_____

_____

_____

_____

_____

_____

_____

_____

_____

Editing

Before you edit your paragraph, complete the following exercises.

Exercise A: Using pronouns

Directions: Fill in the spaces with **my, his, their, he, it,** or **they.**

_____ classmate's name is Beat Sarlos of Zermatt,
   1

Switzerland. When _____ was a child, _____ best friend
                      2   3

was Wilhelm Rizzoli. _____ lived on the same mountain, and
                        4

_____ was about 400 meters high. _____ went to
   5   6

elementary, secondary, and high schools together. _____
                                                      7

parents were also friends, so _____ slept at each other's
                                 8

house very often. _____ favorite activity was skiing; _____
                     9   10

did _____ every day during the winter and spring. To have
      11

fun _____ used to put sticky stuff on the bottom of tourists'
      12

skis so the skis wouldn't slide. When _____ got older,
                                         13

_____ dated girls together every weekend. Today, _____
   14   15

are still good friends, Wilhelm wants to get _____ law
                                                16

degree in the United States, and Beat wants to get _____
                                                       17

medical degree here too.

Exercise B: Using punctuation and verbs

> *Directions:* Punctuate the paragraph below correctly and fill in the correct **past tense** of each verb.

my classmate is fatima sharadi of tehran iran when she (be) _____ a child her best friend (be) _____ masoume abbas fatima and masoume (go) _____ to kindergarten and elementary school together in tehran they also (have) _____ the same piano teacher they (do) _____ many things together they (play) _____ games in the park (sing) _____ songs and (do) _____ their homework together sometimes their families (go) _____ on vacation to the caspian sea together one time they (have) _____ a fight that (last) _____ two years but they (become) _____ friends again after elementary school they (go) _____ to different middle schools high schools and universities today they still write letters and make telephone calls to each other

Exercise C: Using articles

> *Directions:* Complete each sentence with **a, an,** or **the,** or leave the space blank.

1. My classmate is Fatima Sharadi of _____ Tehran, Iran.

2. When she was _____ child, her best friend was _____ Masoume Abbas.

3. Fatima and Masoume went to kindergarten and elementary school together in _____ Tehran.

4. They also had _____ same piano teacher.

5. They did _____ many things together.

6. They played games in _____ park, sang songs, and did their homework together.

7. Sometimes their families went on vacation to _____ Caspian Sea together.

8. After elementary school, they went to _____ different middle schools, high schools, and universities.

9. Today, they still write _____ letters and make _____ telephone calls to each other.

Expanding

Write a letter in English to your best friend. Tell your friend about all the important things that you did last year.

_____

_____

_____

_____

_____

_____

_____

_____

_____

_____

_____

_____

_____

_____

_____

_____

_____

_____

_____

_____

Write about how you spent a special summer.

Look at the picture. What do you think is the relationship between the man and child in the picture? Does this picture remind you of you and your grandparents? Explain why or why not.

Prewriting

Read the following paragraph aloud with your class. Do you think the description is complete? Did the writer tell you what he or she saw? Heard? Felt? Tasted? How could the paragraph be better?

My brother and I used to go to my grandfather's house in the Pyrenees mountains during our summer vacation. He lived in a two-story house beside the Aragon River. He used to wake up every morning at 5:30. Then we got in his small boat, and we went fishing. Usually, we didn't catch many fish, but many mosquitoes caught us. Around 7:00 we stopped fishing, we went back to the house, and my grandmother made breakfast for us. After breakfast, we walked 6 km around a nearby mountain. On our walk we saw many animals such as birds, deer, and rabbits. In the afternoon, my brother and I swam in the river, and my grandparents slept in the house. At night, we all sat beside the river, and my grandfather told funny and scary stories. At 10:00 we went to sleep.

Make the kind of cluster that you think the writer used.

Think about vocabulary. What types of words do you see in the paragraph? Nouns? Verbs? Prepositions? Adjectives? Fill in the blanks on the following chart:

NOUNS	VERBS	PREPOSITIONS	ADJECTIVES
1. _____	_____	_____	_____
2. _____	_____	_____	_____
3. _____	_____	_____	_____
4. _____	_____	_____	_____
5. _____	_____	_____	_____
6. _____	_____	_____	_____
7. _____	_____	_____	_____
8. _____	_____	_____	_____

Talk to two of your classmates. Discuss what you used to do every summer. What unusual things did you do? Did you go to a camp or stay with your grandparents? What activities do you remember the most? Did you do any of the following: swimming, camping, hiking, going to parties, sleeping at friends' houses, studying?

Now make a cluster about how you spent a special summer, or how you used to spend a typical summer. Use as many details as possible to make the reader feel what you felt.

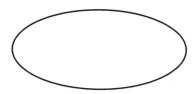

Writing

Use your cluster to write a paragraph. Feel free to make changes as you go. Remember that your teacher will not see this.

_____

_____

_____

_____

_____

_____

_____

_____

_____

_____

_____

_____

_____

Sharing

Read your paragraph very slowly to the entire class. Give everyone a chance to comment on your ideas. What problems do you see? What needs to be changed?

Revising

Using the comments of your classmates, rewrite your paragraph. Make sure your description is clear and complete.

_____

_____

_____

_____

_____

_____

_____

_____

_____

_____

_____

_____

_____

_____

_____

Editing

Complete the following exercises and then edit your paragraph.

Exercise A: Using prepositions

Directions: Fill in the blanks with **beside, of, to, for, in,** or **at.**

When I was a child _____ Algeria, I used to spend
                              1

most _____ my summer vacations _____ the beach.
           2   3

My family lived near Algiers, and my parents often took my

sister and me _____ a beach near Azeffoun. Azeffoun is
                    4

_____ the Mediterranean Sea; it had beautiful white
        5

beaches and warm blue water. _____ course, we swam a
                                      6

lot _____ the beach, and we built a lot _____ sand
         7   8

castles. In addition, we spent many afternoons looking

_____ sea shells and catching small fish. We also played a
        9

special kind _____ racquetball _____ the beach. Now,
                  10   11

it is impossible _____ swim near Azeffoun because the
                      12

army has made it a military base.

Exercise B: Using subordinate clauses

> *Directions:* Change each pair of simple sentences to one complex sentence.

1. We got up in the morning. We went fishing.

   _____

   _____

2. We also played a special kind of racquetball game. We were at the beach.

   _____

   _____

3. My grandfather told funny and scary stories. We sat beside the river.

   _____

   _____

4. We walked around the mountain. We saw many animals.

   _____

   _____

> *Directions:* Fill in the blanks to make complex sentences. Use your imagination.

1. When we went swimming, _____

   _____.

2. _____

   after we _____.

3. While _____,

   _____.

4. _____,

   before I _____.

Exercise C: Correcting sentence order

> *Directions:* Reorder the sentences to show the correct time sequence in the paragraph.

After breakfast, we walked 6 km around a nearby mountain. At 10:00 we went to sleep. Then we got in his small boat, and we went fishing. My brother and I used to go to my grandfather's house in the Pyrenees mountains during our summer vacation. In the afternoon, my brother and I swam in the river, and my grandparents slept in the house. Usually, we didn't catch many fish, but many mosquitoes caught us. At night, we all sat beside the river, and my grandfather told funny and scary stories. He lived in a two-story house beside the Aragon River. On our walk we saw many animals such as birds, deer, and rabbits. He used to wake up every morning at 5:30. Around 7:00 we stopped fishing, we went back to the house, and my grandmother made breakfast for us.

_____

_____

_____

_____

_____

_____

_____

_____

_____

_____

_____

_____

Expanding

Write a paragraph about how your life and interests have changed in the last ten years. Write about six things you *used* to do or like—that you don't anymore. Include such subjects as food, music, clothes, movies, sports or others.

_____

_____

_____

_____

_____

_____

_____

_____

_____

_____

_____

_____

_____

_____

_____

_____

_____

Paragraph 12

Write about your most frightening experience.

Look at the picture. What reaction do you have? Does it make you afraid? Curious? What types of things are you afraid of? Do you ever *enjoy being afraid?* Why do you think people engage in dangerous activities such as sky diving, bungee jumping, extreme skiing, or white water rafting?

Prewriting

Read and discuss the following paragraph about a terrifying plane ride.

My worst experience happened on an airplane about five years ago. It was in the summer. I was flying from Guadalajara to Mexico City. When the plane took off from Guadalajara, the wind was blowing, and it was raining hard. I was a little nervous. The plane was all right for about 30 minutes. I was listening to the music on the airplane's radio. Many people were talking. The stewardesses were serving drinks to the passengers. Suddenly, lightning struck one of the engines. The plane dropped rapidly. Some people were screaming, and the stewardesses were falling down. My heart was beating very fast. I thought I was going to die. But after about 30 seconds, the pilot started the engine. We landed safely. But I will never fly again when the weather is bad.

Notice how the writer makes you feel what happened. What do you see? Hear? Feel?

See _____

_____

_____

_____

Hear _____

_____

_____

Feel _____

_____

_____

Add details to make these sentences from the airplane paragraph more specific. Use your imagination.

> *Example:* My worst experience happened on an airplane about five years ago. (What airplane?) (When, exactly?)

My worst experience happened on <u>a Mexicana DC-7 in August 1995</u>.

1. When the plane took off from Guadalajara, the wind was blowing. (What time of takeoff?) (How fast a wind?)

   _____

   _____

2. I was listening to the music on the airplane's radio. (What kind of music?)

   _____

   _____

3. Suddenly, lightning struck one of the engines. (Which side of the plane?)

   _____

   _____

4. My heart was beating very fast. (About what heart rate?)

   _____

   _____

Think about vocabulary. Use your dictionary to find synonyms of the following words. After you write down the synonyms, orally practice substituting the new words in the sentences in the paragraph on page 102.

1. happened: _____
2. hard: _____
3. nervous: _____
4. talking: _____
5. struck: _____
6. rapidly: _____
7. screaming: _____

Talk to your classmate. Describe something that frightened you. Take turns talking with your classmate about a very frightening experience you each had. Interrupt the person while he or she is talking to ask specific details. Your teacher will show you how to interrupt someone politely to ask for more information.

Think more about the experience that terrified you. Make a cluster of your thoughts, feelings, and observations.

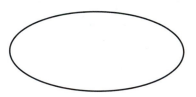

Writing

Change your cluster into a paragraph. Try to explain the situation as clearly as possible. Try to make the reader *feel* the situation.

_____

_____

_____

_____

_____

_____

_____

_____

_____

_____

_____

_____

_____

Sharing

Have another student read your paragraph aloud to you. Do you still feel the fear? Does the paragraph show the fear or excitement that you felt?

Revising

Are there any details that you have forgotten? Is there anything else you saw, heard, or felt? If so, add it to your paragraph now. Make any other changes you like.

_____

_____

_____

_____

_____

_____

_____

_____

_____

_____

_____

_____

_____

_____

Editing

Use the following exercises to help you edit your paragraph.

Exercise A: Using verbs

Directions: The **past continuous tense** is used to show an action in the past that was happening when another action interrupted it. Fill the blanks with the correct form of the **past continuous** or **past tense** of the verbs.

Example: I <u>was eating</u> dinner when the telephone <u>rang</u>.
past continuous   past

My worst experience (happen) _____ in a car on

the night I (graduate) _____ from my high school in

Bangkok, Thailand. I (ride) _____ in my friend Tomo's

car to a party when an accident (happen) _____. We

(go) _____ to pick up our girlfriends when Tomo (lose)

_____ control of the car on a curve. The car (turn)

_____ upside down; as I (look) _____ out the

window, everything (spin) _____ around. We (get)

_____ out of the car fast, but as Tomo (get)

_____ out of the car, he (cut) _____ his leg on

some glass. Because Tomo (bleed) _____ badly, he was

taken to a hospital. Fortunately, I (be) _____ not hurt,

but I never (ride) _____ with Tomo again!

Exercise B: Using punctuation, capitalization, and articles

Directions: Punctuate and capitalize the paragraph. Fill in the spaces with **a, an,** or **the,** or leave the spaces empty.

my worst experience happened on _____ airplane

1

about five years ago it was in _____ summer I was

2

flying from guadalajara to mexico city when _____

3

plane took off from guadalajara _____ wind was

4

blowing and it was raining hard i was _____ little

5

nervous _____ plane was all right for about 30 minutes

6

i was listening to _____ music on _____ airplane's

7   8

radio many people were talking _____ stewardesses

9

were serving drinks to _____ passengers suddenly

10

lightning struck one of _____ engines _____

11   12

plane dropped rapidly some people were screaming and

_____ stewardesses were falling down my heart was

13

beating very fast i though i was going to die but after about

30 seconds _____ pilot started _____ engine we

14   15

landed safely but i will never fly again when _____

16

weather is bad

Exercise C: Understanding complex sentences

> *Directions:* Look at Exercise A. Copy all the **complex sentences** you see.

1. _____

   _____

   _____

   _____

2. _____

   _____

   _____

   _____

3. _____

   _____

   _____

   _____

4. _____

   _____

   _____

   _____

5. _____

   _____

   _____

   _____

6. _____

   _____

   _____

   _____

Expanding

It's time for another class walk around. Find students in the class who are afraid of the items listed below. Then find students who are not afraid. Try to have a short conversation with each person. If a person says he or she is afraid, ask why. If the person is not afraid, ask why not.

	AFRAID	NOT AFRAID
snakes:	_____	_____
tall buildings:	_____	_____
flying on airplanes:	_____	_____
riding roller coasters:	_____	_____
being in closed places:	_____	_____
mice:	_____	_____
lightning:	_____	_____
spiders:	_____	_____
the dark:	_____	_____
guns:	_____	_____
being poor:	_____	_____
driving fast:	_____	_____
heights:	_____	_____

Write about a funny experience you had.

The cats in the picture belong to Marie Ishikawa's American roommate. Do you have a pet? Do people in your country keep cats and dogs inside?

Prewriting

Marie wrote this paragraph about her roommate's cats. How does she describe the cats? Does she like them? Do the cats like her? What do you think about Marie and the cats?

We have three pets in our house. They are Mimi, Molly, and Maggie. They are cats, and they belong to my American roommate. Although they are very smart, they don't understand my language, Japanese. I usually study downstairs every night. The three cats sit on my textbooks. They especially like to use my fat Japanese-English dictionary as a pillow. Sometimes, I tell them to move, but they don't understand my English. One of the cats, Mimi, never listens to me. I have to let her out of the house every morning when I go to school. She never wants to go. I can call her for ten minutes, but she won't come. I used to think that my pronunciation was bad, and that she couldn't understand me. But two days ago, a Japanese friend came to visit me. Her pronunciation is just like mine. She called Mimi, and Mimi ran to her immediately! The problem is not my pronunciation. Mimi and the other cats just want to make fun of me!

   Marie Ishikawa made this cluster before she wrote her paragraph. Fill in the empty places on the cluster with information from the paragraph. What information is not in the paragraph? Do you think that some of the information *not* in the paragraph should be in the paragraph?

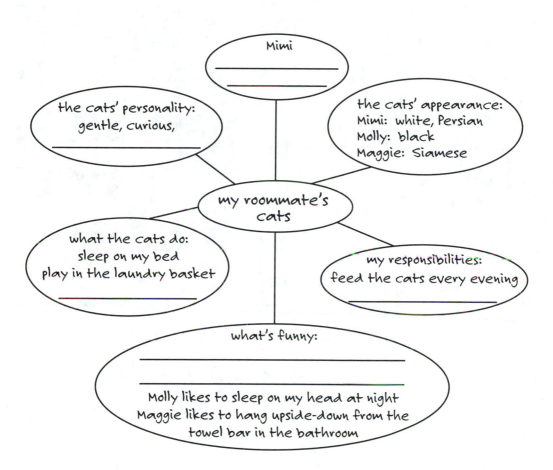

Mimi
_____
_____

the cats' personality:
gentle, curious,
_____

the cats' appearance:
Mimi: white, Persian
Molly: black
Maggie: Siamese

my roommate's cats

what the cats do:
sleep on my bed
play in the laundry basket
_____

my responsibilities:
feed the cats every evening
_____

what's funny:
_____
_____
Molly likes to sleep on my head at night
Maggie likes to hang upside-down from the
towel bar in the bathroom

Think about vocabulary. Fill in the following crossword puzzle.

Across

1. girl-daughter, boy-____
4. past tense of tell
6. preposition: I put the book
   _____ the table.
8. pronoun: The hamburger was
   good, and I ate _____ quickly.
10. part of the face
13. abbreviation of Colorado
14. place to live
16. past participle of do: do, did,
    ___
17. negative word
18. place to cook in a kitchen
20. very large
21. deadly
22. indefinite article:_____ orange
23. a small amount of United States
    money
24. hear
27. preposition: She is ___work.
28. finished
29. pillow covering
33. Same as six Across
34. Comprehend: I don't _____
    what you say.

Down

1. couch
2. preposition: She made an A _____
   her test.
4. pronoun: He gave it to _____.
5. book containing word definitions
7. one, two, _____
9. preposition: He gave it ____ them.
10. abbreviation of California
11. famous character in a movie
12. what you unlock the door with
15. Way of speaking
17. abbreviation for the internet
18. more than "sometimes"
19. abbreviation of Veterans
    Administration
20. exclamation of wonder or surprise
23. an animal you take care of
25. opposite of short
26. a person you like a lot
30. pronoun: Jack and I loaned __ car
    to Susan.
31. Garfield
32. same as 1 Across

Talk with your classmate. Discuss something funny or unusual that has happened to you. Be sure to describe everything specifically. Use these questions to guide you:

When does/did this happen?

Where does/did it happen?

Describe it to me from beginning to end.

Why do/did you think it is/was funny?

Make a cluster about your experience. Be sure to include every important detail.

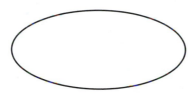

Writing

Write a paragraph using your cluster. Try to communicate the humor in your story.

_____

_____

_____

_____

_____

_____

_____

_____

_____

_____

_____

_____

_____

_____

Sharing

Share your paragraph with another classmate (not the one you talked to before). Is there anything your classmate does not understand? Does your classmate think the story is funny?

Revising

Revise your paragraph. Think about the order of your ideas. Save your most important point for last.

_____

_____

_____

_____

_____

_____

_____

_____

_____

_____

_____

_____

_____

_____

_____

Editing

Think about your paragraph as you do the preposition exercise on the next page.

Exercise A: Using prepositions

Directions: Circle the correct **prepositions** in the paragraph.

It was my first day (in, on, from) this English program. That morning, I had to ride my bike (in, at, to) class (to, on, for) the first time. My host family's father showed me the English program (in, on, around) the map, but I couldn't remember its location. But I got (to, at, on) school OK. After school, (in, on, for) my way home, I got lost. I don't have a sense (in, during, of) direction. First, I was going (on, at, in) the opposite direction, but I didn't realize it. However, I thought the scene was different (from, in, at) what I saw (on, at, in) the morning. I was getting confused, so I asked someone (in, for, on) help. He was very kind and helped me, but soon I got lost again. I asked someone each time I got lost. I asked eight people. (In, Of, During) course, I had a map, but I got lost many times because I couldn't understand English. I had ridden my bicycle (in, for, on) two and a half hours. I thought I would never make it home. I didn't have my host family's telephone number. I tried looking it up, but I didn't know how. I was helpless. I had been (at, on, in) Davis (in, for, on) only two days–it was the second day. I didn't know what to do. I was very tired. I went into an AM-PM store to buy some water. I asked the store clerk one more time. He drew a map, and taught me very kindly. He even took the trouble to go out (in, of, during) the store and point me (in, on, at) the right direction. I arrived home (in, at, on) seven. I want to thank him again. Now, this experience seems like a funny memory!

Now edit your paragraph. When you finish, read the edited paragraph to your class and turn it in to your teacher.

Expanding

Write down a joke that you know (it must be at least 50 words long). Share it with your class. Have a contest to choose the funniest joke.

_____

_____

_____

_____

_____

_____

_____

_____

_____

_____

_____

_____

_____

_____

_____

_____

_____

Paragraph 14

Write about what you are going to do this weekend.

Look at the picture. What do you do on a typical weekend? Do you like to go out or to stay home? What kinds of activities do you enjoy? Do you plan weekends in advance?

Prewriting

Where are you planning to go this weekend? What will you do when you get there? Read the following paragraph silently and answer the questions. Then discuss the paragraph and answers with your class.

This week I am going to go to New York City. On Saturday morning, I am going to see the Statue of Liberty. Next, I am going to visit the United Nations. I want to talk with one of my friends from Myanmar (formerly called Burma), who is in the Myanmar delegation. In the afternoon, I am going to shop on Fifth Avenue. I will buy some shoes for my father, a bag for my mother, and a wallet for my younger brother. In the evening, I really want to go to a baseball game in Yankee Stadium, between the Yankees and the Baltimore Orioles. On Sunday, I am going to spend the morning in Central Park and the afternoon in the Metropolitan Museum of Art. Before I leave, I will send postcards to all of my friends in Rangoon. At about 5:00 P.M., I am going to return to Hartford.

Questions

1. How long is the writer going to stay in New York?

2. Is the writer definitely from Myanmar (Burma)?

3. Is the writer definitely going to the baseball game?

4. What are this person's main interests in going to New York?

5. What are the Yankees and Orioles?

6. What is Hartford?

7. Based on the information in the paragraph, what kind of personality do you think the writer has?

Think about vocabulary. Notice the infinitives and verbs in the paragraph. Fill in the following verb chart:

INFINITIVE	PAST	PAST PARTICIPLE
to go	went	gone
to see		
to visit		
to shop		
to buy		
to spend		
to send		
to return		

Talk to your classmates. Ask about their weekend plans. Where are they going to go? What are they going to do? What will they do on Friday night? Saturday? Sunday? Whom are they going to be with? What do they need to do around the place where they live?

Think about the coming weekend. Where are you going to go? What are you going to do? (Even if you are not sure, imagine that you are.) Make a cluster about your coming activities.

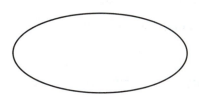

Writing

Exchange clusters with one of your classmates. Write a paragraph based on your classmate's cluster.

_____

_____

_____

_____

_____

_____

_____

_____

_____

_____

_____

_____

_____

_____

Sharing

Give your paragraph to the person whose cluster you used. Take his or her paragraph and read it carefully. What problems do you see? Is the communication clear?

Revising

Rewrite your classmate's paragraph. Make any changes that you feel are appropriate. Try to improve the communication.

_____

_____

_____

_____

_____

_____

_____

_____

_____

_____

_____

_____

_____

_____

_____

Editing

After completing the following exercises, submit your edited paragraph to your teacher.

Exercise A: Using prepositions

> *Directions:* Fill in the spaces with **of, on, in, at, up, to,** or **for.**

Unfortunately, I do not have enough money to travel, so this weekend I am going to stay _____ home. There
1
are many things to do _____ my apartment
2
_____ Saturday. I am going to take my dirty clothes
3
_____ the laundry. After that, I will pick _____
4   5
the junk _____ my apartment. _____ the
6   7
afternoon, I'm going to watch some sports _____ TV.
8
_____ the evening, I will invite a few Sudanese friends
9
_____ my apartment _____ a dinner
10   11
_____ Sudanese shishkebobs. _____ Sunday I
12   13
am going to study _____ my grammar test and go
14
_____ the swimming pool. I think that will take care
15
_____ my weekend.
16

Exercise B: Using subordinate clauses

Directions: In the complex sentences below, put **present tense** in the subordinate clause, and **future tense** (**will** or **going to**) in the independent clause.

Example: (**After**) I will see the Statue of Liberty. I will visit the United Nations.

<u>After I see the Statue of Liberty,</u>   <u>I will visit the United Nations.</u>
         subordinate clause   independent clause

1. (**When**) I am going to shop on Fifth Avenue. I am going to buy some shoes for my father.

   _____

   _____

2. (**After**) I will send some postcards. I will return to Hartford.

   _____

   _____

3. I will go to the swimming pool. (**after**) I am going to study for my grammar test.

   _____

   _____

4. (**Before**) I will pick up the junk in my apartment. I am going to take my dirty clothes to the laundry.

   _____

   _____

Expanding

Below is a map of the world. Divide the class into groups of four. If your group had 1 million dollars to spend, what are five places in the world that you would like to visit for the weekend? Choose the five places, and discuss what you would do in each place. When you finish, tell the rest of the class about your choices.

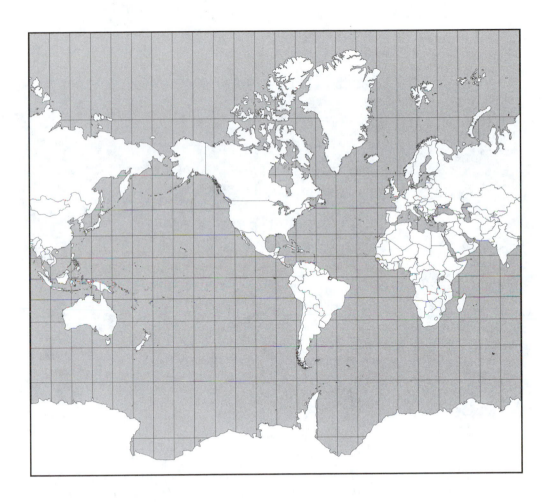

Describe how the world will be in 2100.

Look at the picture. What do you think the scientist is doing? What recent scientific discoveries have you read about? What will happen in the future in medicine? In transportation? In communication? In love? In sports? In economics? In society?

Prewriting

Read the following paragraph and complete the diagram. Discuss the paragraph and the diagram with your class.

What will the world be like in the future? I think that future people will go through the same cycle of life and have the same problems as people today. They will be born. They will go to schools and universities; they will fall in love. They will find jobs. They will grow old and die. But the way of doing these things will be different. Their parents will choose their gender and physical characteristics, and they will be conceived in test tubes. They will have electronic teachers that they see only on TV. They will fall in love through computer dating. They will work at home with computer hook-ups to their jobs. They will grow old with transplanted organs and die when they are 150 years old. Will the world be better? I think there will be less disease, but I think social problems will increase, and war will continue.

Life Cycle ⟶ In Future

choose gender

Birth

Education

Aging/Death

Overall:

Think about vocabulary. Use your dictionary to find the meanings of each of these words from the opening paragraph:

1. cycle: _____

2. characteristics: _____

3. conceived: _____

4. test tubes: _____

5. transplanted: _____

Talk to your classmate. Discuss the future. What do you see in the future? Are you looking forward to it? How will your grandchildren's lives be different from yours? Go back to the categories mentioned at the beginning of this section—medicine, transportation, communication, love, sports, economics, and society—and discuss what you think will happen in 2100.

Make a cluster of your own ideas about the future. Are you optimistic or pessimistic? What do you think will happen to humans and to human society?

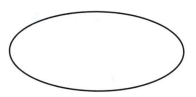

Writing

Try to put your ideas into a paragraph. Concentrate on the ideas and the order of the ideas. Don't worry about grammar.

_____

_____

_____

_____

_____

_____

_____

_____

_____

_____

_____

_____

_____

Sharing

Share your ideas with two of your classmates. What do they think about your predictions? What do you think of theirs? Are there any ideas you would like to change?

Revising

Revise the ideas of your paragraph. Add, subtract, reorder; try to present your ideas as effectively as possible.

_____

_____

_____

_____

_____

_____

_____

_____

_____

_____

_____

_____

Editing

Use the following exercises to help you with your own editing.

Exercise A: Using *that* clauses

Directions: Combine sentences by using a clause with the word **that**.

Example: I think. **(that)** Future people will go through the same cycle of life.

I think that future people will go through the same cycle of life.

1. I think. **(that)** They will have the same problems as people of today.

   _____

2. I believe. **(that)** They will fall in love.

   _____

3. I think. **(that)** They will work at home.

   _____

4. I expect. **(that)** There will be less disease.

   _____

5. I imagine. **(that)** Social problems will increase.

   _____

6. I think. **(that)**

   _____

7. I believe. **(that)**

   _____

8. I imagine. **(that)**

   _____

Exercise B: Using punctuation and capitalization

Directions: Add necessary punctuation and capitalization.

what will the world be like in the future i think that future people will go through the same cycle of life and have the same problems as people today they will be born they will go to schools and universities they will fall in love they will find jobs they will grow old and die but the way of doing these things will be different their parents will choose their gender and physical characteristics and they will be conceived in test tubes they will have electronic teachers that they see only on tv they will fall in love through computer dating they will work at home with computer hook-ups to their jobs they will grow old with transplanted organs and die when they are 150 years old will the world be better i think there will be less disease but i think social problems will increase and war will continue

Exercise C: Using verb tenses

Directions: Fill in each blank with a verb from the following list. Make the verbs **future tense**.

become	fight	be (2)	depend
make	change	have (2)	

I think the world _____ a lot in the future. By
        1

the year 2100, I believe that the strongest countries

_____ Brazil, Canada, Australia, Zaire, Russia, and
        2

possibly Greenland. These countries _____ the
                                              3

most power because of their natural resources. The

industrialized countries of Europe, the United States, and

Japan _____ on these countries for the fuel to
            4

operate their dying technologies. Despite the presence of

nuclear weapons, I believe that countries still

_____ other countries with guns and bombs. The
        5

Middle East still _____ war as it has for 3000 years,
                          6

and, in my opinion, Canada _____ a battlefield
                                      7

because it is between Russia and the United States. I have a

pessimistic view of the future. I think that science

_____ the world worse, and that the twenty-second
        8

century _____ the darkest age of the human spirit.
                9

Expanding

Work with a classmate. Write 10 *yes*-or-*no* questions about the future. Share your questions with your classmates. Ask them how the questions can be improved. Then, ask four people outside your class to answer the questions. Talk to your class about what you find out.

Example: In the future, will scientists find a cure for AIDS?

1. _____?
2. _____?
3. _____?
4. _____?
5. _____?
6. _____?
7. _____?
8. _____?
9. _____?
10. _____?

Write about your last three months.

Look at the picture. Have you skied in the last three months? What are five things that you have done? What are some things you would like to do, but have not done?

Prewriting

Read the following paragraph, and complete the diagram with your class.

I have been in Davis, California, for most of the last three months. During this time, I have done many things. I have visited Old Sacramento. I have skied in the Sierra Mountains and broken my arm, and I have gambled (and lost) a little money in Lake Tahoe casinos. Last month, I spent several days in San Francisco. While I was there, I visited Berkeley and Sausalito. I have visited my younger brother in Los Angeles twice, and last week I had a terrible time in Disneyland. In Davis, I have made many new friends. I have played a lot of tennis, and I have swum almost every day. I have taken many English classes since I have been here, and I have learned a lot of English. I have written many paragraphs in this class.

Now fill in the following diagram.

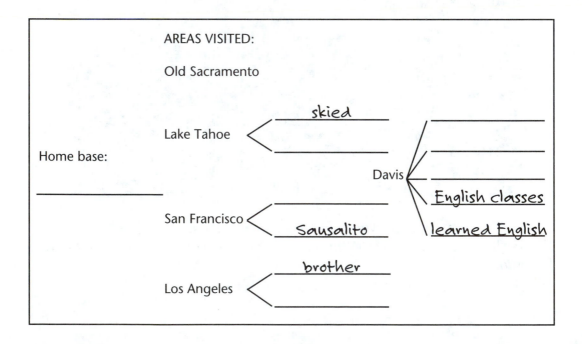

Think about vocabulary. Nine words have been taken from the paragraph and jumbled. Can you figure them out?

Example: ttrienw: _____written_____

1. rreetibl: _____
2. aaarrpphgs: _____
3. ttllie: _____
4. rrohebt: _____
5. nnsite: _____
6. nnasmtoiu: _____
7. sssecal: _____
8. eealnrd: _____
9. nnddyaesli: _____

Talk to your classmate. Discuss the last three months. What has happened to you in your studies? In your job? In your personal life? Where have you gone? What have you seen? Whom have you met? What have you accomplished? What problems have you had? What good things have happened to you?

Cluster your last three months. Try to recall interesting people you have met and things you have done.

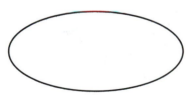

Writing

Transform your cluster into a paragraph. Work on communicating your ideas clearly. Try not to worry about grammar at this point.

_____

_____

_____

_____

_____

_____

_____

_____

_____

_____

_____

_____

_____

_____

Sharing

Exchange paragraphs with three of your classmates. Ask your classmates to circle everything they don't understand. Talk to them about their comments.

Revising

Use the ideas gained from your conversations with your classmates to rewrite your paragraph. Make it stronger and clearer.

_____

_____

_____

_____

_____

_____

_____

_____

_____

_____

_____

_____

_____

_____

Editing

Use the following exercises to help you edit your paragraph.

Exercise A: Using verb tenses

> *Directions:* Fill in the spaces with either the **present perfect** or **past tense**.

I (be) _____ in the United States since
  ___1___

February. First I (live) _____ in Miami; then I (move)
  ___2___

_____ here to Indiana two months ago. Since I (be)
  ___3___

_____ in Bloomington, I (visit) _____
  ___4___   ___5___

Chicago and Indianapolis. In Chicago, I (see) _____
  ___6___

a Chicago Bulls basketball game one night, and the next day I

(go) _____ to the Merchandise Mart. On Memorial
  ___7___

Day, my host family (take) _____ me to the
  ___8___

Indianapolis 500 race, and I (have) _____ a great
  ___9___

time. But mostly, I (stay) _____ in Bloomington. I
  ___10___

(go) _____ to many movies, university plays, and
  ___11___

musical concerts. The weather (be) _____ very
  ___12___

humid so far this summer, but I like Bloomington very much.

Exercise B: Using prepositions and articles

> *Directions:* Fill in the spaces with **for, in, during, since, of, a, an,** or **the**.

I have been _____ Davis, California,

_____ most _____ _____ last
_____2_____   _____3_____   _____4_____

three months. _____ this time, have done many
                          _____5_____

things. I have visited Old Sacramento. I have skied

_____ _____ Sierra Mountains, and I
_____6_____   _____7_____

have gambled _____ little money _____
                        _____8_____   _____9_____

Lake Tahoe casinos. Last month, I spent several days

_____ San Francisco. While I was there, I visited
_____10_____

Berkeley and Sausalito. I have visited my brother

_____ Los Angeles twice, and last week I went to
_____11_____

Disneyland. _____ Davis, I have made many new
                       _____12_____

friends. I have played _____ lot _____
                                       _____13_____   _____14_____

tennis, and I have swum almost every day. I have taken many

English classes _____ I have been here, and I have
                            _____15_____

learned _____ lot _____ English.
                    _____16_____   _____17_____

Exercise C: Recognizing compound sentences

Directions: Study the paragraphs on page 138 and in Exercise A carefully. Write down the eight **compound sentences** you see.

In the paragraph on page 138:

1. _____

_____

2. _____

_____

3. _____

_____

4. _____

_____

In the paragraph in Exercise A:

5. _____

_____

6. _____

_____

7. _____

_____

8. _____

_____

Expanding

Make a list of 10 activities that you have *not* done in the last three months that you would like to do in the next three months. Talk with some of your classmates about your list. Are there any similarities? How will you do the activities that you want to do? Are there any that you can do together with your classmates?

1. _____
2. _____
3. _____
4. _____
5. _____
6. _____
7. _____
8. _____
9. _____
10. _____

17

Write about what makes a good person.

Look at the picture. Does the young woman on the right look like a "good" person? Why or why not? Who is the best person you have ever known (not someone in your family)? Why is that person "good"?

Prewriting

Discuss the following paragraph with your classmates. Do you agree with the writer?

To be well-educated, a person must do five important things. First, she must use her time wisely. She should not watch too much TV, and she should plan her days carefully. Second, she must not limit her studies. She should try to study as many different subjects as she can. For example, if she is a scientist, she should study music, art, and drama. She must see the relationship between different fields. Third, she must have imagination. She must be ready to see what others are unwilling or unable to see. Fourth, she must have self-confidence. She should listen to what others say; however, she must trust herself enough to choose the good from the bad. Fifth, she must never let her curiosity die. She must always look for knowledge, not wait for it to come to her.

Questions

1. The assignment was "Write about what makes a good person." Did the writer follow the assignment? Explain.

   _____

   _____

2. Do you think that the writer emphasizes the intellectual or the emotional aspect of a person? Explain.

   _____

   _____

3. Do you think that the writer would agree with this statement: "Uneducated people are less likely to be 'good' than educated people"? Do you agree? Explain.

   _____

   _____

Think about vocabulary. Many words in English are difficult to define. This chapter is about a "good" person. Write a two-sentence definition of "good." First, try not to look at your dictionary, but afterwards you can get an idea from your dictionary if you want. Compare your definition with those of your classmates.

Talk with your classmates. Discuss good people. First, ask your classmates to give you examples of good people. Is goodness related to education? Religion? Economics? How do people learn to be good?

You are going to write this paragraph with one of your classmates. Together, sit and make a cluster concerning your ideas. Use your experience and what you have learned from parents, reading, or education to write a "prescription" for being a good person.

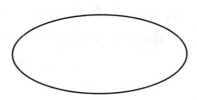

Writing

First, write the paragraph by yourself on a piece of paper. Then talk with your classmate and blend your sentences together into one paragraph.

_____

_____

_____

_____

_____

_____

_____

_____

_____

_____

_____

_____

_____

_____

Sharing

Share your paragraph with another team. Be completely honest. Tell the other team every problem you see in their paragraph.

Revising

With your classmate, revise your paragraph. Try to make it clearer.

_____

_____

_____

_____

_____

_____

_____

_____

_____

_____

_____

_____

_____

_____

_____

Editing

Go over the following exercises with your classmates. See if they give you some ideas for improving your paragraph.

Exercise A: Using forms of verbs

> *Directions:* Choose the right base verb from the list below and fill in the blanks with the correct form of **have to** or **should**.

take   speak   concentrate   read   live   produce

To learn a foreign language completely, a person <u>should</u> <u>concentrate</u> on five important things. First, he _____ 1 in a country in which people use the language. It is more difficult to study a foreign language in a person's native country. Second, the student _____ 2 an organized course of study; just studying alone is not enough. Third, the student _____ 3 on vocabulary and grammar in the classroom because they are the bases of the language. Fourth, the student _____ 4 newspapers, magazines, and books in the language every day, so he can see the language in real situations. Fifth, the student _____ 5 the language every day with native speakers and listen to native speakers on TV and radio every day. These steps _____ 6 a knowledge of the language, if the student works hard.

Exercise B: Using words of transition

Directions: Look back at the paragraph about being well-educated on page 147, and at the sentences in Exercise A about learning a foreign language. Read the paragraph again substituting **to begin with, next, also, in addition,** and **finally** for the words **first, second, third, fourth,** and **fifth.**

Exercise C: Using punctuation and capitalization

Directions: Add the necessary punctuation and capitalization.

to be well educated a person must do five important things first she must use her time wisely she should not watch too much tv and she should plan her days carefully second she must not limit her studies she should try to study as many different subjects as she can for example if she is a scientist she should study music art and drama she must see the relationship between different fields third she must have imagination she must be ready to see what others are unwilling or unable to see fourth she must have self confidence she should listen to what others say however she must trust herself enough to choose the good from the bad fifth she must never let her curiosity die she must always look for knowledge not wait for it to come to her

Now edit your paragraph.

Expanding

Work with a classmate. Imagine that you are going to have a dinner party this weekend with the three "best" people who ever lived. Whom would you invite? Also, it is your responsibility to direct the conversation. What would you talk about with them? Write a conversation between yourselves and the three people in which you discuss a specific topic.

_____

_____

_____

_____

_____

_____

_____

_____

_____

_____

_____

_____

_____

_____

_____

_____

_____

_____

_____

Paragraph

18

Write about your country.

Look at the picture. What do you think are the most interesting things to see in your country: museums, historical places, ancient ruins, mountains, nightclubs, government buildings and monuments, waterfalls and beaches?

Prewriting

Read the following paragraph and complete the diagram. Discuss the paragraph and diagram with your class.

A visitor to my country, Qatar, should visit three towns to get a taste of the country. Traveling from south to north, the traveler should stop at Qatar's main oil terminal, Umm Said. Umm Said is mainly an industrial town with shops, supermarkets, and a golf course for its industrial workers. After he has seen the terminal, the traveler should drive north toward Doha. He will see miles of sandy beaches as he drives along the coast through Wakra, which was once Qatar's most important fishing and pearling village. When he arrives at the capital city of Doha, he will find a large city; eight of every ten Qataris live in Doha. The visitor should walk down the narrow streets of the *souq* to see the ancient trading markets and the people, and he should visit the Qatar National Museum to learn about the country's history. If the visitor goes to Umm Said, Wakra, and Doha, he should get a good picture of the old and new Qatar.

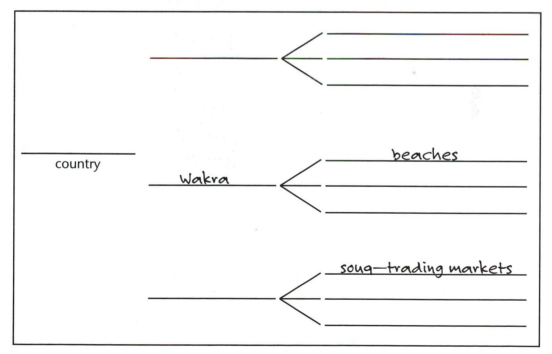

country

Wakra

beaches

souq—trading markets

Think about vocabulary. When you describe your country, you will want to use adjectives. Use a dictionary to find three synonyms for each of the following:

1. interesting: _____ _____ _____
2. beautiful: _____ _____ _____
3. large: _____ _____ _____
4. small: _____ _____ _____
5. important: _____ _____ _____

Talk to a classmate. Discuss her/his country. Ask for one example of each of the following: a beautiful mountain, an excellent beach, a wonderful waterfall, an interesting forest, an unusual geographic point (such as a desert, a canyon, a river), a cool lake, a national park, a great city, a great nightclub, a museum, an ancient ruin, an historical site, a great shopping place, a street with cafés and restaurants.

Imagine that you are a tour guide in your country. What places should a tourist see in order to get a complete picture of your country? Make a cluster of your ideas.

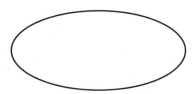

Writing

Exchange your cluster with a classmate. Write a paragraph based on your classmate's cluster.

_____

_____

_____

_____

_____

_____

_____

_____

_____

_____

_____

_____

_____

_____

Sharing

Return the paragraph to the student whose cluster you used. Check the paragraph your classmate wrote on the basis of your cluster. What information did he or she leave out? Is there anything incorrect?

Revising

Revise the paragraph about your country completely. Make the communication clear.

_____

_____

_____

_____

_____

_____

_____

_____

_____

_____

_____

_____

_____

_____

_____

Editing

Use the following exercises to help you edit your paragraph.

Exercise A: Using prepositions and articles.

Directions: Fill in the spaces, or leave them blank if no **preposition** or **article** is required.

_____ visitor _____ Israel should visit
　　　　1　　　　　　　　　　　　2

three important places. Traveling _____ north
　　　　　　　　　　　　　　　　　　　3

_____ south, he should go _____ Lake
　　　4　　　　　　　　　　　　　　　　　　5

Kinneret. _____ Kinneret is _____ beautiful,
　　　　　　　　6　　　　　　　　　　　　　7

fresh-water lake surrounded _____ cool, green hills
　　　　　　　　　　　　　　　　　8

and forests. After he drives through _____ modern
　　　　　　　　　　　　　　　　　　　　9

city _____ Tel Aviv, _____ visitor enters
　　　　10　　　　　　　　　　　　11

_____ desert climate as he nears Jerusalem. While he
　　12

is _____ Jerusalem, he should mainly visit
　　　13

_____ old city, where he will see Moslems, Christians,
　　14

and Jews living _____ an area thousands of years old.
　　　　　　　　　15

He should shop _____ the Arabic market near
　　　　　　　　　16

_____ Damascus Gate, and he should visit
　　17

_____ Mosque _____ Omar, _____
　　18　　　　　　　　　19　　　　　　　　　20

Via Dolorosa, and _____ Wailing Wall. After he stays
　　　　　　　　　21

_____ Jerusalem _____ a few days, he should
22   23

drive through _____ desert _____ the Dead
24   25

Sea where he can climb Masada. If the visitor sees

_____ Kinneret, Jerusalem, and _____ Dead
26   27

Sea, he should get _____ interesting look
28

_____ my country.
29

Exercise B: Using subordinate clauses

Directions: Make **complex sentences** from the pairs of sentences below.

1. He has seen the oil terminal. The traveler should drive north toward Doha.

   _____

   _____

2. He arrives in Doha. He will find a large city.

   _____

   _____

3. He leaves Tel Aviv. The visitor enters a desert climate.

   _____

   _____

4. He is in Jerusalem. He should visit the old city.

   _____

   _____

Exercise C: Using adjectives

> *Directions:* Fill in each blank with an **adjective** to make the
> sentence more descriptive.

1. Umm Said is mainly an industrial town with _____
   shops, _____ supermarkets, and a _____ golf
   course for its industrial workers.
2. He will see miles of _____ white beaches as he drives
   along the _____ coast.
3. After he has seen the _____ terminal, the traveler should
   drive north toward Doha.
4. He should shop in the _____ Arabic market.
5. After he stays in Jerusalem for a few days, he should drive
   through the _____ desert to the Dead Sea.
6. If the visitor sees the _____ Kinneret, _____
   Jerusalem, and the _____ Dead Sea, he should get an
   interesting look at my country.

Expanding

Choose a country in the world that you have never been to. Find some information about that country and take your class on a tour of interesting places in it. Be sure to include at least 10 specific places to visit in the country you choose.

1. _____

2. _____

3. _____

4. _____

5. _____

6. _____

7. _____

8. _____

9. _____

10. _____

Write about the person you want to marry, or to whom you are married.

Look at the picture. Is this like a typical wedding picture from your country? How long does the process of marriage usually take (from falling in love to wedding day)? Discuss the marriage process with your class. Who arranges the wedding ceremony, and who pays for it?

Prewriting

What kind of person would you like to marry (or did you marry)? What characteristics are important to you in a spouse? Or maybe you do not want to marry. Read and discuss this paragraph with your class.

I want to get married to another Peruvian when I am 24 years old. Now I will describe the kind of man I want to marry. First, he should come from a good Peruvian family. Second, he should be about two years older than I, about 26. Third, he must look good. I want him to have black hair and a big body. Fourth, he should be smart. He must have a university education. Fifth, I hope he will have a good job in a big city. For example, I would like to marry a doctor in Lima. Sixth, and most important, he must have a kind personality. I think this kind of man will make a good husband and a good father.

Now complete the following diagram.

1. Good family

2. _____ age _____ = _____

3. _____ < black hair
          _____

4. _____ = university education

5. _____ Occupation _____ < _____
                                 _____

6. _____ < _____
          _____

Think about vocabulary. Match the following marriage-related words with their definitions:

1. engagement	A. dress worn by woman at the marriage ceremony
2. groom	B. the woman getting married
3. reception	C. official document certifying the marriage
4. bride	D. female friend or relative of the woman getting married
5. wedding	E. get married
6. bridesmaid	F. party after the marriage ceremony
7. tie the knot	G. clothing worn by men at the marriage ceremony
8. marriage license	H. the man getting married
9. tuxedo	I. the marriage ceremony
10. wedding gown	J. period of time after a man and woman agree to get married

Talk to your classmate. Discuss the kind of person you want to marry—or the person to whom you're married. Have you ever met someone like that? What qualities are important to you: intelligence, looks, personality, interests? At what age do you want to (or did you) get married? Do (did) you want to marry someone older or younger or the same age? Would you marry someone who is divorced? Would you marry someone who is not from your country? Would you marry someone who is not from your race? Do you think that people should marry partners who have the same interests—or different interests? Do you want to marry at all? If not, why not?

Make a cluster about your ideal spouse. (If you are already married, make a cluster of the characteristics you admire in your spouse.)

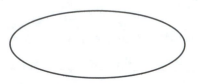

Writing

Write a paragraph based on your cluster. Try to concentrate on your ideas; don't worry about grammar at this point.

_____

_____

_____

_____

_____

_____

_____

_____

_____

_____

_____

_____

_____

Sharing

Read your paragraph to a classmate. What does your classmate think about it? Work on the communication of ideas. Are all your ideas present? Have they been communicated clearly?

Revising

Revise your paragraph. When you are satisfied, give your paragraph to your classmate, and ask for his or her paragraph in return. Revise this paragraph also, changing whatever you like. Compare your revisions with your classmate's.

_____

_____

_____

_____

_____

_____

_____

_____

_____

_____

_____

_____

_____

Editing

Use the following exercises to help you edit your paragraph.

Exercise A: Using articles

> *Directions:* Fill in the spaces with **a, an,** or **the**, or leave them blank.

I think _____ right age for me to get married is 28. I
                  1

want to marry _____ woman who is about 23. First, she
                  2

should have _____ good personality. I want _____ wife
                  3   4

who is _____ sweet and kind to children. Second, she should
           5

be _____ intelligent. I don't care if she has _____ university
       6   7

degree, but I want her to have _____ open mind. Third, I
                                    8

want her to be _____ beautiful woman. She should be
                    9

_____ little shorter than I, and I hope she will have _____
   10   11

brown hair and _____ green eyes. I'm sure my future wife
                    12

will not be like _____ woman I have described, but I hope
                      13

so!

Exercise B: Using relative clauses

Directions: Change the second sentence to a **relative clause** and add it to the first sentence.

Example: I will choose a man. He will be about five years older than I. **(who)**

I will choose a man who will be about five years older than I.

1. I want a wife. She will be kind to children. **(that)**

_____

_____

2. I want a husband. He will like to work around the house. **(who)**

_____

_____

3. My husband will be a smart man. He has a college degree. **(who)**

_____

_____

4. My future wife will be from my city. This city is in Turkey. **(which)**

_____

_____

Exercise C: Using punctuation and capitalization

Directions: Add the necessary punctuation and capitalization.

i want to get married to another peruvian when i am 24 years old now i will describe the kind of man i want to marry first he should come from a good peruvian family second he should be about two years older than i about 26 third he must look good i want him to have black hair and a big body fourth he should be smart he must have a university education fifth i hope he will have a good job in a big city for example i would like to marry a doctor in lima sixth and most important he must have a kind personality i think this kind of man will make a good husband and a good father

Expanding

Conduct an intercultural research project. Find seven people from different countries (or just seven people if this is not possible)—from both inside and outside the class. Ask them to rate the following items in order of importance when choosing a spouse.

Have them number the items from 1 to 9: 1 = most important and 9 = least important.

	Person						
Characteristic	1	2	3	4	5	6	7
Physical appearance							
Religion							
Family							
Intelligence/education							
Personality							
Age							
Health							
Interests							
Race/nationality							

After you have completed your research, write a short paragraph that summarizes the results. Present your findings to the class.

Paragraph

20

Write about your life at age 75.

Look at the pictures. What are your ideas about old age? How old is "old"? Which of the pictures look like those of typical "older" people? Which of the people would you like to be like?

Prewriting

Can you imagine your life at age 75? What will it be like? Read and discuss the following paragraph with your class.

> When I am 75 years old, I would like to be healthy, to live comfortably, and to have a nice family. I would not like to be like many old people. I hope that I will stay in good condition because I would like to swim, jog, and play tennis regularly. Also I would like to have enough money to live easily, not too much and not too little. I would like to have a large house on the beach and a nice car. I hope that I will not have to live on money from the government or from my children. Most important, I'd like to have a good family with three or four grandchildren to play with. I'd like to have a good reputation, with the respect of myself and the people who know me.

What are four things the writer of this paragraph is concerned about.

1. _____
   _____

2. _____
   _____

3. _____
   _____

4. _____
   _____

How much money do you think the writer believes is "enough money to live easily"?

What do you think the writer believes is "a nice car"?

What do you think the writer believes is "a good family"?

Think about vocabulary. There are many words in English that refer to age. How would you define each of the following? Compare your definitions with those of your classmates:

infant:	_____
child:	_____
teenager:	_____
young person:	_____
middle-aged person:	_____
old person:	_____
senior citizen:	_____
elderly person:	_____

Talk to a classmate. Imagine your old age. What do you want to be like when you are 75? What do you want your family to be like? How many grandchildren would you like to have? How much money would you like to have? What kinds of activities would you like to be doing: playing sports, traveling around the world, staying at home reading? Ask your classmate these and more questions.

Cluster your own desires about life at age 75. What ideas come to mind? What kind of life do you want?

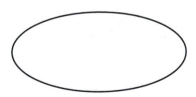

Writing

Use your cluster to write a paragraph. Remember: clear ideas, clear communication. Make changes as you write if you wish.

_____

_____

_____

_____

_____

_____

_____

_____

_____

_____

_____

_____

_____

Sharing

Read your paragraph to the entire class, and ask for comments. Is there anything you left out? Is there anything your classmates don't understand?

Revising

Rewrite your paragraph, making it stronger and clearer. Make as many changes as you want.

_____

_____

_____

_____

_____

_____

_____

_____

_____

_____

_____

_____

_____

_____

Editing

Complete the following exercises.

Exercise A: Using verb tenses

> *Directions:* Change the verb from **would like** to **hope that** plus the **future tense**.

> *Example:* I would not like to live like many old people.

> <u>I hope that I will not live like many old people.</u>

1. I would like to be able to swim.

_____

2. I would like to have enough money to live easily.

_____

3. I would like to have a nice family.

_____

4. I would like to have a good reputation.

_____

Exercise B: Using punctuation and capitalization

Directions: Add the necessary punctuation and capitalization.

when i am 75 years old i would like to be healthy to live comfortably and to have a nice family i would not like to be like many old people i hope that i will stay in good condition because i would like to swim jog and play tennis regularly also i would like to have enough money to live easily not too much and not too little i would like to have a large house on the beach and a nice car i hope that i will not have to live on money from the government or from my children most important i'd like to have a good family with three or four grandchildren to play with i'd like to have a good reputation with the respect of myself and the people who know me

Exercise C: Using infinitives

> *Directions:* From the list below, choose **an infinitive** to put into each sentence.

to have	to get	to play	to spend	to lead
to go	to watch	to drink	to meet	to visit

At this time of my life, I would like _____ most of
1

my time with my friends and family in my native Toledo. In

the mornings, I'd like _____ up at 5:00 A.M. Then I
2

would like _____ a cup of strong coffee, and read and
3

write for a few hours before I go to oversee my vineyards. Like

my grandfathers before me, I would like _____ to the
4

bullfights on summer afternoons. Afterwards, I would like

_____ my friends in our favorite café, and I would like
5

_____ cards, dominoes, and chess with them. And I
6

would like _____ the beautiful Toledan sunsets with a
7

glass of my vineyard's red wine in my hand and my family at

my side. In the evenings, I'd like _____ friends and
8

have them visit me. Then at 10:00 P.M., I would like

_____ a big dinner with my family, smoke a cigar, and
9

drink a little sherry. I hope that I will be able _____
10

this kind of life, and I think that I will.

Now edit your paragraph.

Expanding

Many people are healthy, happy, and productive well into their eighties and nineties. Find or think of examples of such people, and write a paragraph about them. Who were they? What did they achieve? When did they achieve those things?